TWENTIETH CENTURY INTERPRETATIONS
OF

RICHARD II

TWENTIETH CENTURY INTERPRETATIONS
OF

RICHARD II

A Collection of Critical Essays

Edited by

PAUL M. CUBETA

Prentice-Hall, Inc. *Englewood Cliffs, N.J.*

A SPECTRUM BOOK

For Beth

and

With Gratitude To
Eric Kolvig

and

Kennedy Furey

© 1971 by Prentice-Hall, Inc., Englewood Cliffs, New Jersey. A SPECTRUM BOOK. All rights reserved. No part of this book may be reproduced in any form or by any means without permission in writing from the publisher. ISBN: C–0–13–780874–7; P–0–13–780866–6. *Library of Congress Catalog Card Number* 70–178029. Printed in the United States of America.

10 9 8 7 6 5 4 3 2 1

PRENTICE-HALL INTERNATIONAL, INC. (*London*)
PRENTICE-HALL OF AUSTRALIA, PTY. LTD. (*Sydney*)
PRENTICE-HALL OF CANADA, LTD. (*Toronto*)
PRENTICE-HALL OF INDIA PRIVATE LIMITED (*New Delhi*)
PRENTICE-HALL OF JAPAN, INC. (*Tokyo*)

Contents

c.1

Introduction

by Paul M. Cubeta

I

Efforts to categorize Shakespeare's plays by genre have a tidy sense of failure about them. The first published Quarto (1597) called *Richard II* a tragedy; the first collected edition of Shakespeare's plays, the First Folio of 1623, entitled it *The Life and Death of Richard II*. Today it is identified as the first of the second tetralogy of history plays which includes the Henriad— *1 Henry IV*, *2 Henry IV* and *Henry V* (1597–1599). The years surrounding the composition of *Richard II* (1594–1596) were extraordinarily productive ones for the playwright, just turned thirty, and he probably was not so concerned as his later critics whether *A Midsummer Night's Dream* was a pastoral or a comedy; *Romeo and Juliet* a romance or a tragedy; *The Merchant of Venice* a tragedy or a comedy. What mattered to him was that in his newly-formed Lord Chamberlain's Company he had as fine a group of players as Polonius ever introduced to Elsinore: "The best actors in the world, either for tragedy, comedy, history, pastoral, pastoral-comical, historical-pastoral, tragical-historical, tragical-comical-historical-pastoral."

From the unspectacular achievement of his first plays, the chronicle histories, *1, 2, 3 Henry VI* (1590–1592), Shakespeare seems to have discovered that a confusing multiplicity of historical characters—Yorkists and Lancastrians intriguing for power during the Wars of the Roses (1455–1485)—does not make for compelling drama. In *Richard III* (1593), the final play of this first tetralogy, he learned from the drama of his predecessors Kyd and Marlowe that dramatic action and stage convention find their clearest focus, not in historical events, but in a dominant character. Two years later he was drawn back to explore the historical antecedents of the Wars of the Roses and to raise questions about the nature of kingship and of nations, but this time not by creating a villain-king in the conventional role of the Machiavel, as he had done in *Richard III*. The new play, *Richard II*, went far beyond its immediate sources (Raphael Holinshed's *Chronicles of England, Scotland, and Ireland*; Samuel Daniel's *The First Four Books of the Civil Wars Between the Two Houses of Lancaster and York;* an anonymous play entitled *Woodstock;* and a poem by many hands relating the downfall of several great princes, among them Richard, which was called *A Mirror for Magistrates)* and grappled directly with the inner meanings of regicide.

Like his contemporaries Shakespeare believed that history could teach moral and political lessons. For orthodox, conservative Elizabethans the historical process, stated and restated in the works just cited, was a manifestation of divine will. Their concern for national unity and identity, for the maintenance of order in the commonweal, and for the consequences of revolution became obsessive as they watched the years of the Tudor dynasty wane with the waning Eliza-beth, who was to die childless in 1603, surrounded by many who would have liked to be her heir. These contemporary anxieties had been largely shaped a hundred years earlier when the first Tudor, Henry VII, commissioned Polydore Virgil to compose a history of England which would give sanction to the insecure Tudor claim to the throne at the end of the Wars of the Roses. The arguments of Virgil and other Tudor historians like Edward Hall and Holinshed demonstrated that God had worked out His perfect plan for His chosen country England through the providential accession of Henry VII, whose grand-daughter would be the great Elizabeth herself. According to these religious and political assumptions, now known as the "Tudor Myth," the deposition of Richard II, who had reigned by "divine right," was not just a political revolution by which an unpopular, ineffectual Plantagenet king was overthrown by powerful feudal lords led by Henry Bolingbroke, Duke of Hereford and Lancaster, but a sin against God. Because England countenanced this usurpation, she had to suffer as penance almost one hundred years of civil war following Richard's murder in 1399. But England, God's "New Israel," was ultimately forgiven when the Lancastrian, Henry of Richmond (the Henry VII mentioned above), slew the Yorkist Richard III at the battle of Bosworth Field in 1485 and brought peace and prosperity to England by uniting the warring houses of York and Lancaster through his marriage to Elizabeth of York. Such was the meaning of English history from 1399 to 1485 as the Tudor historians presented it. One hundred and ten years later, as the old queen failed, Elizabethan England wondered whether this cycle of history was to begin all over again with a similar chaos of usurpation and civil war. Yeats' question in "The Second Coming" would have seemed to Shakespeare's contemporaries menacingly real: "And what rough beast, its hour come round at last/ Slouches toward Bethlehem to be born?"

In an effort to encourage Englishmen to identify Elizabeth with

Richard II, supporters of her former favorite, the Earl of Essex, per-
suaded Shakespeare's company to perform the play two days before
the abortive Essex rebellion of February 7, 1601. Although it may be
difficult today to see *Richard II* as a revolutionary document, some
of Shakespeare's contemporaries did, among them the Queen herself,
who was never fond of it—more, one suspects, for political than for
literary reasons. Probably for fear of offending royal sensibilities and
thus incurring censorship, the deposition scene of Act IV was never
published during the Queen's lifetime. Shortly after the execution of
Essex, Elizabeth is reported to have said to William Lambard: "I am
Richard II know ye not that?" Lambard replied: "Such a wicked imagination was determined and attempted by a most unkind Gent. the
most adored creature that ever your Majestie made"—i.e., Essex,
whose fortune Elizabeth had indeed made. The Queen answered:
"He that will forget God, will also forget his benefactors; this tragedy
was played 40^{tie} times in open streets and houses." [1] What Lambard
here recalls is that Essex was entrusted with the chief command of
the Queen's troops in putting down the Irish rebellion of 1599, abused
his power, conspired with the rebel leader, and, when recalled to
London, moved to seize the throne—an act of treason which to Elizabeth was a sin against God as well as a betrayal of her trust and love.
In placing the security of her throne ahead of her personal affection
and sending Essex to his death, Elizabeth must have recognized the
irony of being identified with the irresponsible Richard II, whose
realm was "swarming with caterpillars" (III, iv, 47), rather than with
the Gardener's ideal monarch who would do as she had done:

> . . . like an executioner,
> Cut off the heads of too fast growing sprays
> That look too lofty in our commonwealth.
>
> (III, iv, 33–35)

II

Whatever historical parallels may have been read into Shakespeare's
play by his contemporaries or whatever political calculations may have
motivated a particular performance, Shakespeare did not write *Richard II* as historian or politician or theologian. The Tudor myth serves
his dramatic purposes, not his political biases, and the myths he gener-

---

[1] Matthew W. Black, *A New Variorum Edition of Shakespeare: The Life and
Death of King Richard the Second* (Philadelphia and London: J. B. Lippincott Co.,
1955), p. 582.

ates within it are far richer in their historical and human implications than anything Polydore Virgil could devise or Essex's followers seize on. Thus in his apocalyptic vision of a perfect England (II, i, 40–67), the dying Gaunt sings first of a country transcending time, an ideal mythic place where man and nature fulfill God's highest purposes: "This other Eden, demi-paradise." After nineteen lines undulating in crescendos of praise for that unfallen world, the longest subject of any Shakespearean sentence collapses in the barren predicate of "Is now leased out, I die pronouncing it,/ Like to a tenement or pelting farm. . . ." Gaunt's final judgment that "England . . . hath made a shameful conquest of itself" leaves ambiguous the question of moral and political responsibility, and ambiguous it remains. Throughout the play Richard's disorder, as one cause, is set against Bolingbroke's disobedience as another. But however caused, the note of loss sounds everywhere. It is heard in Gaunt's farewell to his king, his country, and his life. It is struck even earlier (I, ii) by the Duchess of Gloucester as she departs for Plashy "with her companion grief":

> Desolate, desolate, will I hence and die:
> The last leave of thee takes my weeping eye.
>
> (I, ii, 73–74)

These, the Duchess's last words in the play, anticipate the Queen's first:

> Yet I know no cause
> Why I should welcome such a guest as grief,
> Save bidding farewell to so sweet a guest
> As my sweet Richard. . . .   (II, ii, 6–10)

Departures, farewells, pilgrimages in exile, banishments from "this earth of majesty" mark the lives of every character and establish a pervasive elegiac tone. The lists at Coventry, which were to have witnessed a formal trial by combat between Mowbray and Bolingbroke, fade into a scene of "ceremonious leave/ And loving farewell of our several friends" as the two exiles begin their "long and weary pilgrimage" (I, iii, 48–51). Richard's departure for Ireland hastens his own fall, for at home his loyal troops disperse:

> Farewell: our countrymen are gone and fled,
> As well assured Richard their king is dead.
>
> (II, iv, 16–17)

Even his apostrophe of joyous reunion dissolves quickly into an elegy on the mortality of kings—"and farewell king" (III, ii, 170). The play draws to a close, as it began, with exiles and tearful farewells:

> Good sometime queen, prepare thee hence for France:
> Think I am dead and that even here thou takest,
> As from my death-bed, thy last living leave.
>
> (V, i, 37–39)

Moreover, *Richard II* offers no assurance of a brave new world once Henry IV has seized power. Henry banishes Exton, Richard's murderer, from "this other Eden": "With Cain go wander thorough shades of night" (V, v, 43). He vows a pilgrimage to the Holy Land "to wash this blood off from my guilty hand" (50), but Lady Macbeth could have advised him of the futility of the gesture. He can no longer cry out for "justice and rough chastisement" to revenge the murder of his uncle Gloucester, whose blood was shed "like sacrificing Abel's" (I, i, 104, 106). On the contrary, he has—"in God's name" (IV, i, 113) —ascended the royal throne by usurpation and the murder of God's anointed. England, saved from economic bankruptcy, has fallen into moral bankruptcy. The Lancastrians cannot restore Gaunt's lost demi-paradise, nor will they ever be, like some of their predecessors,

> Renowned for their deeds as far from home,
> For Christian service and true chivalry,
> As is the sepulchre in stubborn Jewry
> Of the world's ransom, blessed Mary's son.
>
> (II, i, 53–56)

Although Bolingbroke on his return to England speaks of his fortune ripening as he moves toward his carefully unstated goal of kingship— "till my infant fortune comes to years" (II, iii, 66)—there is little sense of victorious fulfillment or of a nation redeemed at the end of the play. The many metaphors of falling and rising do not suggest any final political stasis. The play concludes, not in a triumphant forward movement of history, but with Henry IV reenacting unawares the gestures and ritual acts of two weeping women, Richard's Queen and the Duchess of Gloucester, who mourn for their lost world as he mourns for a time when he had not the King's blood on his conscience.

Thus Bolingbroke in power only returns the cycle of the drama to its beginnings. Act IV opens with an inquiry into Gloucester's death which leads to another knightly confrontation, uglier and less ceremonious than the one in I, i. Gloucester's murder is made to serve Bolingbroke's political purposes in this scene as it did Richard's in Act I. Again the trial is postponed. It is not justice that Bolingbroke seeks but political persecution; it is not Gloucester's death that concerns him, but loyalty to the new regime:

Little are we beholding to your love,
And little look'd for at your helping hands.
(IV, i, 160–161)

Earlier in the drama Northumberland had defended his rebellion
against a "most degenerate king" (II, i, 262) in "this declining land"
(240); "Reproach and dissolution" hung over Richard, he claimed
(258), because he was "basely led/ By flatterers" (241–242). At the end
Bolingbroke confronts anxieties of a similar sort: he grieves because
his own heir—"young wanton and effeminate boy"—is "as dissolute
as desperate" (V, iii, 10, 20). *Dissolute, dissolve, desperate, despair, degenerate, depressed, dishonor, depart, discharge, disperse, depose, decline, divide, debase*—the language of *Richard II* is heavy with words
that in this politically and morally disintegrating world foreshadow
the cry of Hamlet's father: "O Hamlet, what a falling-off was there"
(*Ham.,* I, v, 47).

III

Although regal styles and personalities change, although attitudes
toward the sanctions of political power differ, the rhythm of events
in *Richard II* suggests that there has been no revolution in human
affairs or in the human spirit. The play is constructed as a series of
public confrontations that dissolve without resolution only to recur.
Many critics point to the conflicts that arise between religious and
political stances, between tragedy and history, drama and politics,
words and actions, or between the ideal and the real, shadow and
substance; but one does not find here the tragic conflicts of good and
evil. E. M. W. Tillyard sees in this play a contrast between two ways
of life, Medieval and Renaissance, past and present: "the world of
medieval refinement . . . is threatened and in the end superseded by
the more familiar world of the present." According to Irving Ribner,
Richard II argues "better a strong and efficient king with illegal title"
than a "weak and effeminate king" of undisputed title. He observes a
tension between private and public virtues, between a sympathetic
failure and an unheartwarming success. For Peter Ure the design of
the struggle is "unarmed and deficient majesty versus armed and able
usurpation." Brents Stirling points out the conflict in the characters
of the double protagonists: "Bolingbroke's realism, self-containment,
and resourcefulness" opposed to "Richard's romantic defeatism, near-
hysteria, and pathetic reliance upon others." Jan Kott locates the
dilemma in the inevitable dichotomy where "there is only the king's
situation, and the system. . . . In Shakespeare's world there is a con-

tradiction between the order of action and the moral order. This contradiction is human fate."

The essential conflict in the play, however, is one that shows Shakespeare the way to the tragic vision of *Hamlet* and *King Lear*: the
engagement of Richard with himself. In later Shakespearean tragedy
the world is created before the hero enters. Here, the hero is the
creator of his world; indeed he wants to be the writer, director, and
leading actor of his play—roles which Hamlet will better understand.
The movement from pageant in Act I to prison in Act V reveals how
Richard's perceptions of himself and his world change as he confronts
two moments of personal danger. In the beginning, he moves with
serene confidence as he covers political intrigue with ceremonious
ritual and administers justice with formal rhetorical flourishes empty
of content. He enjoys playing king, delights in his capricious adjudi-
cation of the encounter between two peers, Mowbray and Bolingbroke.
He knows that he is king by divine right, God's vicegerent, "His deputy
anointed in His sight" (I, ii, 38), in a world permanently ordered by
traditional loyalties, even though his cynical political machinations
implicate him in the murder of his uncle, the Duke of Gloucester. As
Alvin Kernan puts it,

> In that Edenic world which Gaunt described and Richard destroyed,
> every man knew who he was. His religion, his family, his position in so-
> ciety, his assigned place in processions large and small, his coat of arms,
> his traditional duties, and even his clothing, which was then prescribed
> by sumptuary laws, told him who he was and what he should do and
> even gave him the formal language in which to express this socially-
> assigned self. But once, under the pressures of political necessity and
> personal desires, the old system is destroyed, the old identities go with it.

Gaunt, who knows who he is and what he has become, can pun on
his name even on his deathbed; Bolingbroke, who knows who he is
and what he will become, seeks his patrimony and his name—Lancaster—and finds them and more. For Richard, who has understood
himself as king and man only in terms of "respect/ Tradition, form,
and ceremonious duty" (III, ii, 172–173), the search for identity and
self-knowledge is an unexpected and lonely descent, rather different
from the kingly role-playing with which from his throne at the Coventry lists he prepares to be rid of all political threats: "We will descend
and fold him in our arms" (I, iii, 54). His return from Ireland is the
occasion for another descent and moment of extravagant posturing:
"Dear earth, I do salute thee with my hand . . ." (III, ii, 6). When
Richard learns of Bolingbroke's growing power and the dispersal of
his own troops, he can only invoke the empty security of the royal
name, symbol without substance: "I had forgot myself: am I not king?

. . . Is not the king's name twenty thousand names?/ Arm, arm, my name!" (III, ii, 83, 85–86). Richard's actions and words remain a tangle of contradictions. When military decisions are called for, he urges his comrades to "sit upon the ground" so that he may sing elegiacally of the death of kings. Even before the Gardener divines his downfall (III, iv, 19), he foretells as a biographer of kings his own deposition and murder and prophesies the career of his successor—"Some haunted by the ghosts they have deposed" (III, ii, 158). Later, with keener political acumen, he will warn Northumberland of his forthcoming doom at the hands of a fearful Henry (V, i, 55–68).

Richard's use of the traditional medieval conceit of the Court of Death anticipates the prison at Pomfret, for Death too is a poet-playwright permitting kings "a little scene,/ To monarchize" before the castle walls of the actor's own flesh are penetrated by his pin. His humbling recognition of death's power leads to the acknowledgment that both mortal king and frail man are subjects: "subjected thus/ How can you say to me, I am a king?" (176–177). The question is a rhetorical one, for it is Richard himself who has declared his divine kingship, "the deputy elected by the Lord" (57): "am I not king?" (83). Both at Flint Castle and Westminster Hall the issue is not merely whether Richard deposes himself but whether he can attain a new integrity of character by uniting myth and action, symbol and reality, public gesture and private necessity.

IV

For a time in Westminster Hall Richard seems concerned only with directing the actors at his abdication. He gains a perverse enjoyment from the embarrassment and bewilderment he causes Bolingbroke by identifying stage direction with political action:

> Here, cousin, seize the crown;
> Here, cousin:
> On this side my hand, and on that side yours.
> (IV, i, 181–183)

As at Flint Castle he declares that, deposed, stripped, and bankrupt, he is still king of his griefs (191–193). But a new definition of a private kingship is emerging, for with eyes full of tears, he can now acknowledge his own guilt: "I find myself a traitor with the rest" (248). He is Judas as well as Christ because he has betrayed his symbolic kingship. "The king body natural becomes a traitor to the king body politic." [2] Playing fondly on *care* as *responsibility* and *grief* in a way reminiscent of Gaunt's puns on *gaunt*, Richard recognizes that to be undone as king does not dissolve his personal anguish at the loss of "my glories and my state" (192). When Bolingbroke baldly asks, "Are you contented to resign the crown?" (200), Richard can only respond:

> Ay, no; no, ay; for I must nothing be;
> Therefore no no, for I resign to thee.
> (201–202)

The quibble on ay-no is not merely an indication of Richard's irresolution; it is the only statement of his identity now possible. Richard is "unking'd" (220); he has "no name, no titles" (255); his face is "bankrupt of his majesty" (267). What difference what King Richard wills, since as king he is nothing: "I am no, so no is ay"? But the double negative "therefore no no" (202) becomes a way of not saying "no." Richard will make of his undoing, forswearing, and forgoing a gesture of affirmation for himself as a man with tears, hands, tongue, and breath. Although his act lacks the tragic profoundity of Lear's mad stripping on the heath—"Thou art the thing itself: unaccommodated man is no more but such a poor, bare, forked animal as thou art" (*KL*, III, iv, 100–101)—he moves in this ceremonious resignation of ceremony to the moment when, after seeing his face in the mirror, he can acknowledge the limits of play, manners, appearances, and even words. The "brittle glory" of majesty—Richard's kingly self—lies shattered on the floor of Westminster Abbey, destroyed by himself as "king of griefs." What started as another flamboyant theatrical gesture, like his throwing down of his warder at the lists of Coventry, moves to an insight deeper than he could have anticipated. Ironically the "silent king" Henry affords the opportunity for Richard's tragic awareness when he modifies the moral of Richard's sport—"How soon my sorrow hath destroy'd my face" (291)—to "The shadow of your sorrow hath destroy'd/ The shadow of your face" (292–293). Bolingbroke sees only the pretense or appearance of sorrow and the fractured reflection of a face. But the remark leads Richard to turn from surface images of kingship, too long his only concern, and to seek instead an inward illumination and a new sense of identity as man:

[2] It was a concept of medieval political law that a king possessed two bodies, one human and one divine: his natural body as a man and his immortal kingship, a mystic political body deified by God's grace. Ernst H. Kantorowicz, *The King's Two Bodies: A Study in Mediaeval Political Theology* (Princeton: Princeton University Press, 1957), p. 39.

> 'Tis very true, my grief lies all within;
> And these external manners of laments
> Are merely shadows to the unseen grief
> That swells with silence in the tortured soul;
> There lies the substance.   (295–299)

Like Hamlet, who wishes that "this too too sullied flesh would melt/ Thaw, and resolve itself into a dew" (*Ham.*, I, ii, 129–130), Richard recognizes that he possesses "that within which passeth show—/ These but the trappings and the suits of woe" (*Ham.*, I, ii, 85–86). Substance is no longer the shows of grief that have marked much of Richard's descent but rather the silence in the tortured soul of a suffering man. Although it is not within Richard's capacity to declare with Hamlet "the rest is silence" or even with Cordelia "love, and be silent," he has learned "the way/ How to lament the cause" (301–302). In that ambiguous silence lies any final explanation of his grief. Is he now aware of his failure as king and as man, of his sins against God and England? Or is he grieving over the political circumstances that drove him to his inevitable abdication, a man believing, as Lear does, that he is more sinned against than sinning? Is his sorrow born of humiliation or humility?

Richard's descent ends in the lonely confines of Pomfret, its "flinty ribs" and "ragged prison walls" (V, v, 20–21) reminiscent of the "rude ribs" and "tatter'd battlements" (III, ii, 32, 52) of Flint Castle, where he began his debasing pilgrimage. Without an audience, Richard finds solace in a soliloquy on the nature of artistic creation, an act which might be looked on as a surrogate for the creating of a legitimate heir for the throne of England. Richard now reviews his roles in the kingdom of his mind and pronounces them all failures: "Thus play I in one person many people,/ And none contented" (31–32). King, beggar, nothing—Richard perceives the immensity of a fall that can end only in his death. As music plays about him, perhaps symbolic of the harmonies of the unfallen world that are yet audible in the music of the spheres, he acknowledges his violation of divine order and the retribution which has befallen him: "I wasted time, and now doth time waste me" (49).

Richard's murder explodes upon the play as an extraordinary act of violence, the only moment of bloody, physical brutality in the play. Traversi calls it "a pedestrian piece of melodrama"; Ure is torn between viewing it as "courageous" or "perhaps perfunctory." But these judgments overlook the fact that the play opened with thwarted efforts to revenge the death of Gloucester, cut down by "murder's bloody axe" (I, ii, 21). Because Gaunt will not "lift/ An angry arm against His minister" (40–41), the Duchess of Gloucester cries, "call it not patience, Gaunt; it is despair" (29). The wheel of history again swings full circle as Henry's assassins like Richard's rid each king in turn of a "living fear" (V, iv, 2). Divine retribution is once more only political murder.

In Act I Richard had dramatized his royal will by imposing it abruptly on knights appellant in armor accompanied by trumpet fanfares and heralds "appointed to direct these fair designs" (I, iii, 45). At the hour of his death he can find only a "poor groom" of his stable (V, v, 72), whom he ironically calls his "noble peer" (67), a discourteous prison keeper—"that sad dog/ That brings me food to make misfortune live" (70–71)—armed servants, and a disloyal knight. In the emerging world of the Lancastrians "law and form and due proportion,/ Showing, as in a model, our firm estate" (III, iv, 41–42), are irrevocably lost, and even Richard's horse Barbary, "created to be awed by man" (91), mocks the old models by proudly bearing a usurper. Richard endured "the badges of his grief and patience" (V, ii, 33) as he rode to his abdication behind the "hot and fiery steed" (8) that Bolingbroke was mounted on. Now, however, he can no longer tolerate "this all-hating world" (V, v, 66), where even "this music mads me" (61) and where efforts to hammer out a new world of the mind's making collapse with the knowledge that

> Nor I nor any man that but man is
> With nothing shall be pleased, till he be eased
> With being nothing.   (39–41)

When the keeper prudently refuses what should have been only the ceremonious gesture of tasting the royal plate, the king in his most human moment turns in rage and beats the man whose only fault is obedience to the new order: "Patience is stale, and I am weary of it" (103). Richard's cry is more than Hamlet's anguished lament: "How weary, stale, flat, and unprofitable/ Seem to me all the uses of this world" (*Ham.*, I, ii, 133–134). Richard in furious anger proves the meaning of his name—"strong and powerful like a ruler"—as his queen said he must:

> The lion dying thrusteth forth his paw,
> And wounds the earth, if nothing else, with rage
> to be o'erpowered. . . .   (V, i, 29–31)

There is nothing now of the passive martyrdom of the betrayed Christ that made Richard a king of griefs at Westminster Hall. Scoffing and grinning Death will not have the satisfaction of boring through this castle wall "with a little pin" (III, ii, 169). Wielding an axe, not a warder nor a scepter, Richard can die affirming a truer royalty:

Mount, mount, my soul! Thy seat is up on high;
Whilst my gross flesh sinks downward, here to die.

(V, v, 112–113)

All of the political and equestrian metaphors of mounting and falling
are resolved in Richard's dying declaration of his double identity.
The soul of a divinely anointed king mounts to its high throne; the
mortal body of the man sinks downward to stain in blood "the king's
own land" (111). Exton is right to declare Richard "as full of valour
as of royal blood" (114). Like Hamlet he has proved most royal.

The Historical Richard

by Irving Ribner

Medieval political theory regarded the king as responsible to the lords of the realm as well as to God, as King John had been forced to acknowledge in signing Magna Carta; medieval kings were not considered to be responsible to God alone, as was Shakespeare's Queen Elizabeth, for this was a Renaissance political doctrine which was not asserted in England until the coming of the Tudors. Historically the deposition of Richard II occurred in a medieval, feudal context, and not in the later Tudor absolutist terms of Shakespeare's play.

The historical Richard II was the grandson of King Edward III who ruled England from 1327 to 1377, outliving by less than a year his eldest son, Edward the Black Prince, famous for his conquests in France. Richard, son of the Black Prince, succeeded his grandfather at the age of eleven, and England was ruled for him by the eldest of his surviving uncles, John of Gaunt, Duke of Lancaster. During the Peasants' Revolt of 1381 the young king behaved with great courage, himself stabbing the rebel Wat Tyler. When Gaunt left to fight in Spain, the regency passed to Thomas of Woodstock, Earl of Gloucester, the sixth son of Edward III, who seems to have been a cruel and scheming politician anxious to secure the throne for himself, rather than the "plain well-meaning soul" that Shakespeare makes of him.

As Richard grew older he gathered about him a court party of favourites who opposed Gloucester and his supporters, including Gaunt's son, Henry Bolingbroke and Thomas Mowbray, Earl of Nottingham and later Duke of Norfolk. These men seized some of Richard's followers and had them summarily executed. In 1389 Richard declared himself of age and ready to rule England by himself. Gloucester was forced to give up his regency; but he did so unwillingly, refusing to recognize that Richard was of age and continuing to intrigue against the crown. For several years Richard seems to have ruled competently, even effecting a reconciliation with the Lords who had followed Gloucester. As Gloucester's intrigues became more insupportable, he was kidnapped by Richard's agents, conveyed to the English stronghold of Calais in France and there murdered. Historically, Mowbray had nothing to do with this death, which seems to have been engineered by one Lapoole, but for the purpose of his play Shakespeare combines these two historical figures.

After the death of his Queen, Anne of Bohemia, Richard married Isabella of France. He gathered new favourites about him and by various unscrupulous financial schemes which alienated his subjects he raised money to support a luxurious and extravagant court. In 1398 Bolingbroke and Mowbray quarrelled, and at this point Shakespeare's play begins. Upon the return of Bolingbroke from exile to regain the estates Richard had unlawfully seized from him, Richard was deposed by the lords of the realm who had deserted him in favour of Bolingbroke, who now became King Henry IV. Since the deposed king soon became a rallying point for all of those who opposed the new regime, in 1400 Richard was murdered at Pontefract (Pomfret) Castle in Yorkshire.

Richard II

by E. M. W. Tillyard

Of all Shakespeare's plays *Richard II* is the most formal and ceremonial. It is not only that Richard himself is a true king in appearance, in his command of the trappings of royalty, while being deficient in the solid virtues of the ruler; that is a commonplace: the
ceremonial character of the play extends much wider than Richard's
own nature or the exquisite patterns of his poetic speech.

First, the very actions tend to be symbolic rather than real. There
is all the pomp of a tournament without the physical meeting of the
two armed knights. There is a great army of Welshmen assembled to
support Richard, but they never fight. Bolingbroke before Flint
Castle speaks of the terrible clash there should be when he and
Richard meet:

> Methinks King Richard and myself should meet
> With no less terror than the elements
> Of fire and water, when their thundering shock
> At meeting tears the cloudy cheeks of heaven.

But instead of a clash there is a highly ceremonious encounter leading to the effortless submission of Richard. There are violent challenges before Henry in Westminster Hall, but the issue is postponed.
The climax of the play is the ceremony of Richard's deposition. And
finally Richard, imprisoned at Pomfret, erects his own lonely state
and his own griefs into a gigantic ceremony. He arranges his own
thoughts into classes corresponding with men's estates in real life;
king and beggar, divine, soldier, and middle man. His own sighs
keep a ceremonial order like a clock:

> Now, sir, the sound that tells what hour it is
> Are clamorous groans, which strike upon my heart,

> Which is the bell: so sighs and tears and groans
> Show minutes, times, and hours.

Second, in places where emotion rises, where there is strong mental action, Shakespeare evades direct or naturalistic presentation and resorts to convention and conceit. . . . Emotionally Richard's parting from his queen could have been a great thing in the play: actually it is an exchange of frigidly ingenious couplets.

> *Rich.* Go, count thy way with sighs; I mine with groans.
> *Qu.* So longest way shall have the longest moans.
> *Rich.* Twice for one step I'll groan, the way being short,
> And piece the way out with a heavy heart.

This is indeed the language of ceremony not of passion. Exactly the same happens when the Duchess of York pleads with Henry against her husband for her son Aumerle's life. Before the climax, when York gives the news of his son's treachery, there had been a show of feeling; but with the entry of the Duchess, when emotion should culminate, all is changed to prettiness and formal antiphony. This is how the Duchess compares her own quality of pleading with her husband's:

> Pleads he in earnest? look upon his face;
> His eyes do drop no tears, his prayers are jest;
> His words come from his mouth, ours from our breast:
> He prays but faintly and would be denied;
> We pray with heart and soul and all beside:
> His weary joints would gladly rise, I know;
> Our knees shall kneel till to the ground they grow:
> His prayers are full of false hypocrisy;
> Ours of true zeal and deep integrity.

And to "frame" the scene, to make it unmistakably a piece of deliberate ceremonial, Bolingbroke falls into the normal language of drama when having forgiven Aumerle he vows to punish the other conspirators:

> But for our trusty brother-in-law and the abbot,
> And all the rest of that consorted crew,
> Destruction straight shall dog them at the heels.

The case of Gaunt is different but more complicated. When he has the state of England in mind and reproves Richard, though he can be rhetorical and play on words, he speaks the language of passion:

> Now He that made me knows I see thee ill.
> Thy death-bed is no lesser than thy land

> Wherein thou liest in reputation sick.
> And thou, too careless patient as thou art,
> Commit'st thy anointed body to the cure
> Of those physicians that first wounded thee.
> A thousand flatters sit within thy crown,
> Whose compass is no bigger than thy head.

But in the scene of private feeling, when he parts from his banished son, both speakers, ceasing to be specifically themselves, exchange the most exquisitely formal commonplaces traditionally deemed appropriate to such a situation.

> Go, say I sent thee for to purchase honour
> And not the king exil'd thee; or suppose
> Devouring pestilence hangs in our air
> And thou art flying to a fresher clime.
> Look, what thy soul holds dear, imagine it
> To lie that way thou go'st, not whence thou com'st.
> Suppose the singing birds musicians,
> The grass whereon thou tread'st the presence strew'd,
> The flowers fair ladies, and thy steps no more
> Than a delightful measure or a dance;
> For gnarling sorrow hath less power to bite
> The man that mocks at it and sets it light.

Superficially this may be maturer verse than the couplets quoted, but it is just as formal, just as mindful of propriety and as unmindful of nature as Richard and his queen taking leave. Richard's sudden start into action when attacked by his murderers is exceptional, serving to set off by contrast the lack of action that has prevailed and to link the play with the next of the series. His groom, who appears in the same scene, is a realistic character alien to the rest of the play and serves the same function as Richard in action.

Thirdly, there is an elaboration and a formality in the cosmic references, scarcely to be matched in Shakespeare. These are usually brief and incidental, showing indeed how intimate a part they were of the things accepted and familiar in Shakespeare's mind. But in *Richard II* they are positively paraded. The great speech of Richard in Pomfret Castle is a tissue of them: first the peopling of his prison room with his thoughts, making its microcosm correspond with the orders of the body politic; then the doctrine of the universe as a musical harmony; then the fantasy of his own griefs arranged in a pattern like the working of a clock, symbol of regularity opposed to discord; and finally madness as the counterpart in man's mental kingdom of discord or chaos. Throughout the play the great common-

place of the king on earth duplicating the sun in heaven is exploited
with a persistence unmatched anywhere else in Shakespeare. Finally
(for I omit minor references to cosmic lore) there is the scene (III. 4)
of the gardeners, with the elaborate comparison of the state to the
botanical microcosm of the garden. But this is a scene so typical of the
whole trend of the play that I will speak of it generally and not
merely as another illustration of the traditional correspondences.

The scene begins with a few exquisitely musical lines of dialogue
between the queen and two ladies. She refines her grief in a vein of high
ceremony and sophistication. She begins by asking what sport they can
devise in this garden to drive away care. But to every sport proposed
there is a witty objection.

> *Lady.* Madam, we'll tell tales.
> *Queen.* Of sorrow or of joy?
> *Lady.*   Of either, madam.
> *Queen.* Of neither, girl:
>   For if of joy, being altogether wanting,
>   It doth remember me the more of sorrow;
>   Or if of grief, being altogether had,
>   It adds more sorrow to my want of joy.
>   For what I have I need not to repeat,
>   And what I want it boots not to complain.

Shakespeare uses language here like a very accomplished musician doing exercises over the whole compass of the violin. Then there enter
a gardener and two servants: clearly to balance the queen and her
ladies and through that balance to suggest that the gardener within
the walls of his little plot of land is a king. Nothing could illustrate
better the different expectations of a modern and of an Elizabethan
audience than the way they would take the gardener's opening words:

> Go, bind thou up yon dangling apricocks,
> Which, like unruly children, make their sire
> Stoop with oppression of their prodigal weight.

The first thought of a modern audience is: what a ridiculous way for
a gardener to talk. The first thought of an Elizabethan would have
been: what is the symbolic meaning of those words, spoken by this
king of the garden, and how does it bear on the play? And it would
very quickly conclude that the apricots had grown inflated and over-
weening in the sun of the royal favour; that oppression was used with
a political as well as a physical meaning; and that the apricots
threatened, unless restrained, to upset the proper relation between
parent and offspring, to offend against the great principle of order.

And the rest of the gardener's speech would bear out this interpretation.

> Go thou, and like an executioner
> Cut off the heads of too fast growing sprays,
> That look too lofty in our commonwealth.
> All must be even in our government.
> You thus employ'd, I will go root away
> The noisome weeds, which without profit suck
> The soil's fertility from wholesome flowers.

In fact the scene turns out to be an elaborate political allegory, with the Earl of Wiltshire, Bushy, and Green standing for the noxious weeds which Richard, the bad gardener, allowed to flourish and which Henry, the new gardener, has rooted up. It ends with the queen coming forward and joining in the talk. She confirms the gardener's regal and moral function by calling him "old Adam's likeness," but curses him for his ill news about Richard and Bolingbroke. The intensively symbolic character of the scene is confirmed when the gardener at the end proposes to plant a bank with rue where the queen let fall her tears, as a memorial:

> Rue, even for ruth, here shortly shall be seen
> In the remembrance of a weeping queen.

In passing, for it is not my immediate concern, let me add that the gardener gives both the pattern and the moral of the play. The pattern is the weighing of the fortunes of Richard and Bolingbroke:

> Their fortunes both are weigh'd.
> In your lord's scale is nothing but himself
> And some few vanities that make him light;
> But in the balance of great Bolingbroke
> Besides himself are all the English peers,
> And with that odds he weighs King Richard down.

For the moral, though he deplores Richard's inefficiency, the gardener calls the news of his fall "black tidings" and he sympathises with the queen's sorrow. And he is himself, in his microcosmic garden, what neither Richard nor Bolingbroke separately is, the authentic gardener-king, no usurper, and the just represser of vices, the man who makes "all even in our government.". . . Though Richard himself is a very important part of the play's ceremonial content, that content is larger and more important than Richard. With that caution, I will try to explain how the ritual or ceremonial element in *Richard II* differs from that in the earlier History Plays, and through such an explanation to conjecture a new interpretation of the play. . . . *Richard II,*

with all the emphasis and the point taken out of the action, we are
invited, again and again, to dwell on the sheer ceremony of the various
situations. The main point of the tournament between Bolingbroke
and Mowbray is the way it is conducted; the point of Gaunt's parting
with Bolingbroke is the sheer propriety of the sentiments they utter;
the portents, put so fittingly into the mouth of a Welshman, are more
exciting because they are appropriate than because they precipitate an
event; Richard is ever more concerned with how he behaves, with the
fitness of his conduct to the occasion, than with what he actually does;
the gardener may foretell the deposition of Richard yet he is far more
interesting as representing a static principle of order; when Richard
is deposed, it is the precise manner that comes before all—

> With mine own tears I wash away my balm,
> With mine own hands I give away my crown,
> With mine own tongue deny my sacred state,
> With mine own breath release all duty's rites.

We are in fact in a world where means matter more than ends, where
it is more important to keep strictly the rules of an elaborate game than
either to win or to lose it.

Now though compared with ourselves the Elizabethans put a high
value on means as against ends they did not go to the extreme. It was
in the Middle Ages that means were so elaborated, that the rules of the
game of life were so lavishly and so minutely set forth. *Richard II* is
Shakespeare's picture of that life.

Of course it would be absurd to suggest that Shakespeare pictured
the age of Richard II after the fashion of a modern historian. But
there are signs elsewhere in Shakespeare of at least a feeling after historical verity; and there are special reasons why the age of Richard II
should have struck the imaginations of the Elizabethans. . . .

But there were other reasons why the reign of Richard II should
be notable. A. B. Steel, his most recent historian, begins his study by
noting that Richard was the last king of the old medieval order:

> the last king ruling by hereditary right, direct and undisputed, from the
> Conqueror. The kings of the next hundred and ten years . . . were
> essentially kings *de facto* not *de jure,* successful usurpers recognised after
> the event, upon conditions, by their fellow-magnates or by parliament.

Shakespeare, deeply interested in titles as he had showed himself to be
in his early History Plays, must have known this very well; and Gaunt's
famous speech on England cannot be fully understood without this
knowledge. He calls England

> This nurse, this teeming womb of royal kings,
> Fear'd by their breed and famous by their birth,

Renowned for their deeds as far from home,
For Christian service and true chivalry,
As is the sepulchre in stubborn Jewry
Of the world's ransom, blessed Mary's son.

Richard was no crusader, but he was authentic heir of the crusading Plantagenets. Henry was different, a usurper; and it is with reference to this passage that we must read the lines in *Richard II* and *Henry IV* which recount his desire and his failure to go to Palestine. That honour was reserved for the authentic Plantagenet kings. Richard then had the full sanctity of medieval kingship and the strong pathos of being the last king to possess it. Shakespeare probably realised that however powerful the Tudors were and however undisputed their hold over their country's church, they had not the same sanctity as the medieval kings. He was therefore ready to draw from certain French treatises, anti-Lancastrian in tone, that made Richard a martyr and compared him to Christ and his accusers to so many Pilates giving him over to the wishes of the London mob. Shakespeare's Richard says at his deposition:

Though some of you with Pilate wash your hands,
Showing an outward pity; yet you Pilates
Have here deliver'd me to my sour cross,
And water cannot wash away your sin.

Holy and virtuous as the Earl of Richmond is in *Richard III*, he does not pretend to the same kingly sanctity as Richard II. Such sanctity belongs to a more antique, more exotically ritual world; and Shakespeare composed his play accordingly.

Not only did Richard in himself hold a position unique among English kings, he maintained a court of excessive splendour. Froissart writes as follows in the last pages of his chronicle:

This King Richard reigned king of England twenty-two year in great prosperity, holding great estate and signory. There was never before any king of England that spent so much in his house as he did by a hundred thousand florins every year. For I, Sir John Froissart, canon and treasurer of Chinay, knew it well, for I was in his court more than a quarter of a year together and he made me good cheer. . . . And when I departed from him it was at Windsor; and at my departing the king sent me by a knight of his, Sir John Golofer, a goblet of silver and gilt weighing two mark of silver and within it a hundred nobles, by the which I am as yet the better and shall be as long as I live; wherefore I am bound to pray to God for his soul and with much sorrow I write of his death.

But Shakespeare need not have gone to Froissart for such information. In an age that was both passionately admiring of royal magnificence

and far more retentive of tradition than our own the glories of
Richard's court must have persisted as a legend. Anyhow that Shakespeare was aware of them is plain from Richard's address to his own
likeness in the mirror:

> Was this face the face
> That every day under his household roof
> Did keep ten thousand men?

The legend must have persisted of this court's continental elegance, of
the curiosities of its dress, of such a thing as Anne of Bohemia intro-
ducing the custom of riding side-saddle, of Richard's invention of the
handkerchief for nasal use. Then there were the poets. Shakespeare
must have associated the beginnings of English poetry with Chaucer
and Gower; and they wrote mainly in Richard's reign. There must
have been much medieval art, far more than now survives, visible in
the great houses of Elizabeth's day, illuminated books and tapestry;
and it would be generally associated with the most brilliant reign of
the Middle Ages. Finally in Richard's reign there was the glamour of
a still intact nobility: a very powerful glamour in an age still devoted
to heraldry and yet possessing an aristocracy who, compared with the
great men of Richard's day, were upstarts.

All these facts would have a strong, if unconscious, effect on Shakespeare's mind and induce him to present the age of Richard in a
brilliant yet remote and unrealistic manner. He was already master of
a certain antique lore and of a certain kind of ceremonial writing: it
was natural that he should use them, but with a different turn, to do
this particular work. Thus he makes more solemn and elaborates the
inherited notions of cosmic correspondences and chivalric procedure
and he makes his ritual style a central and not peripheral concern.
Hence the portentous solemnity of the moralising gardeners, the powerful emphasis on the isolated symbol of the rue-tree, the elaborate
circumstances of the tournament between Bolingbroke and Mowbray,
and the unique artifice of Richard's great speeches: speeches which are
the true centre of the play but central with a far wider reference than
to the mere character of Richard.

In speaking of medieval illuminated books and tapestry I do not
wish to imply anything too literal: that Shakespeare had actual examples of such things in mind when he wrote *Richard II*. But it is true
that many passages in this play call them up and that unconscious
memory of them *might* have given Shakespeare help. Take a passage
from one of Richard's best known speeches.

> For God's sake, let us sit upon the ground
> And tell sad stories of the death of kings:

> How some have been depos'd, some slain in war,
> Some haunted by the ghosts they have depos'd,
> Some poison'd by their wives, some sleeping kill'd;
> All murder'd: for within the hollow crown
> That rounds the mortal temples of a king
> Keeps Death his court, and there the antic sits,
> Scoffing his state and grinning at his pomp,
> Allowing him a breath, a little scene,
> To monarchise, be fear'd, and kill with looks,
> Infusing him with self and vain conceit,
> As if this flesh which walls about our life
> Were brass impregnable, and, humour'd thus,
> Comes at the last and with a little pin
> Bores through his castle wall, and farewell king!

Critics have seen a reference here to the *Mirror for Magistrates,* but Chaucer's *Monk's Tale* would suit much better. Death, keeping his court, is a pure medieval motive. Still, these motives were inherited and need imply nothing unusual. But Death the skeleton watching and mocking the king in his trappings is a clear and concrete image that reminds one of the visual arts: and above all the exquisiteness, the very remoteness from what could have happened in an actual physical attempt, of someone boring through the castle wall with a little pin precisely recaptures the technique of medieval illumination. Before the tournament Bolingbroke prays God:

> And with thy blessings steel my lance's point
> That it may enter Mowbray's waxen coat.

That again is just like medieval illumination. When a wound is given in medieval art there is no fusion of thing striking with thing stricken; the blow simply rests in a pre-existing hole, while any blood that spouts out had pre-existed just as surely. This is the kind of picture called up by Mowbray's "waxen coat." . . .

The case for the essential medievalism of *Richard II* is even stronger when it is seen that the conspirators, working as such, do not share the ceremonial style used to represent Richard and his court. Once again the usual explanation of such a contrast is too narrow. It has been the habit to contrast the "poetry" of Richard with the practical common sense of Bolingbroke. But the "poetry" of Richard is all part of a world of gorgeous tournaments, conventionally mournful queens, and impossibly sententious gardeners, while Bolingbroke's common sense extends to his backers, in particular to that most important character, Northumberland. We have in fact the contrast not only of two characters but of two ways of life.

One example of the two different ways of life has occurred already: in the contrast noted between the mannered pleading of the Duchess of York for Aumerle's life and Henry's vigorous resolve immediately after to punish the conspirators. The Duchess and her family belong to the old order where the means, the style, the embroidery matter more than what they further or express. Henry belongs to a new order, where action is quick and leads somewhere. But other examples are needed to back up what to many readers will doubtless seem a dangerous and forced theory of the play's significance. First, a new kind of vigour, the vigour of strong and swift action, enters the verse of the play at II. I. 224, when, after Richard has seized Gaunt's property and announced his coming journey to Ireland, Northumberland, Ross, and Willoughby remain behind and hatch their conspiracy. Northumberland's last speech especially has a different vigour from any vigorous writing that has gone before: from the vigour of the jousters' mutual defiance or York's moral indignation at the king's excesses. After enumerating Bolingbroke's supporters in Brittany, he goes on:

> All these well furnish'd by the Duke of Brittain
> With eight tall ships, three thousand men of war,
> Are making hither with all due expedience
> And shortly mean to touch our northern shore:
> Perhaps they had ere this, but that they stay
> The first departing of the king for Ireland.
> If then we shall shake off our slavish yoke,
> Imp out our drooping country's broken wing,
> Redeem from broken pawn the blemish'd crown,
> Wipe off the dust that hides our sceptre's gift
> And make high majesty look like itself,
> Away with me in post to Ravenspurgh.

The four lines describing by different metaphors how the land is to be restored are not in a ritual manner but in Shakespeare's normal idiom of Elizabethan exuberance. It is not for nothing that the next scene shows the Queen exchanging elegant conceits about her sorrow for Richard's absence with Bushy and Green. But the largest contrast comes at the beginning of the third act. It begins with a very fine speech of Bolingbroke recounting to Bushy and Green all their crimes, before they are executed. It has the full accent of the world of action, where people want to get things and are roused to passion in their attempts:

> Bring forth these men.
> Bushy and Green, I will not vex your souls
> (Since presently your souls must part your bodies)

> With too much urging your pernicious lives,
> For 'twere no charity.

That is the beginning, and the speech goes on to things themselves not to the way they are done or are embroidered. And when at the end Bolingbroke recounts his own injuries it is with plain and understandable passion:

> Myself a prince by fortune of my birth,
> Near to the king in blood, and near in love
> Till you did make him misinterpret me,
> Have stoop'd my neck under your injuries
> And sigh'd my English breath in foreign clouds,
> Eating the bitter bread of banishment.

The scene is followed by Richard's landing in Wales, his pitiful inability to act, and his wonderful self-dramatisation. As a display of externals, as an exaltation of means over ends (here carried to a frivolous excess), it is wonderful; yet it contains no lines that for the weight of unaffected passion come near Bolingbroke's single line,

> Eating the bitter bread of banishment.

The world for which Bolingbroke stands, though it is a usurping world, displays a greater sincerity of personal emotion.

Thus *Richard II,* although reputed so simple and homogeneous a play, is built on a contrast. The world of medieval refinement is indeed the main object of presentation but it is threatened and in the end superseded by the more familiar world of the present.

In carrying out his object Shakespeare shows the greatest skill in keeping the emphasis sufficiently on Richard, while hinting that in Bolingbroke's world there is the probability of development. In other words he makes the world of Bolingbroke not so much defective as embryonic. It is not allowed to compete with Richard's but it is ready to grow to its proper fulness in the next plays. This is especially true of the conspirators' characters. Hotspur, for instance, is faintly drawn yet in one place he speaks with a hearty abruptness that shows his creator had conceived the whole character already. It is when Hotspur first meets Bolingbroke, near Berkeley Castle. Northumberland asks him if he has forgotten the Duke of Hereford, and Hotspur replies:

> No, my good lord, for that is not forgot
> Which ne'er I did remember: to my knowledge
> I never in my life did look on him.

At the beginning of the same scene Northumberland's elaborate compliments to Bolingbroke show his politic nature: it is the same man who at the beginning of *2 Henry IV* lies "crafty-sick." Bolingbroke too is consistent with his later self, though we are shown only certain elements in his character. What marks out the later Bolingbroke and makes him a rather pathetic figure is his bewilderment. For all his political acumen he does not know himself completely or his way about the world. And the reason is that he has relied in large part on fortune. Dover Wilson remarked truly of him in *Richard II* that though he acts forcibly he appears to be borne upward by a power beyond his volition. He is made the first mover of trouble in the matter of the tournament and he wants to do something about Woodstock's murder. But he has no steady policy and having once set events in motion is the servant of fortune. As such, he is not in control of events, though by his adroitness he may deal with the unpredictable as it occurs. Now a man who, lacking a steady policy, begins a course of action will be led into those "by-paths and indirect crook'd ways" of which Henry speaks to his son in *2 Henry IV*. Shakespeare says nothing of them in *Richard II,* but they are yet the inevitable result of Henry's character as shown in that play. It is worth anticipating and saying that Prince Hal differs from his father in having perfect knowledge both of himself and of the world around him. Of all types of men he is the least subject to the sway of fortune. . . .

Richard II thus at once possesses a dominant theme and contains within itself the elements of those different things that are to be the theme of its successors.

It must not be thought, because Shakespeare treated history, as described above, in a way new to him that he has lost interest in his old themes. On the contrary he is interested as much as ever in the theme of civil war, in the kingly type, and in the general fortunes of England. And I will say a little on each of these before trying to sum up the play's meaning in the tetralogy to which it belongs.

Richard II does its work in proclaiming the great theme of the whole cycle of Shakespeare's History Plays: the beginning in prosperity, the distortion of prosperity by a crime, civil war, and ultimate renewal of prosperity. The last stage falls outside the play's scope, but the second scene with the Duchess of Gloucester's enumeration of Edward III's seven sons, her account of Gloucester's death, and her call for vengeance is a worthy exordium of the whole cycle. The speeches of the Bishop of Carlisle and of Richard to Northumberland . . . are worthy statements of the disorder that follows the deposition of the rightful king. In doctrine the play is entirely orthodox. Shakespeare knows that Richard's crimes never amounted to tyranny and hence that outright rebellion against him was a crime. He leaves uncertain the question of who murdered Woodstock and never says that Richard was personally responsible. The king's uncles hold perfectly correct

opinions. Gaunt refuses the Duchess of Gloucester's request for vengeance, the matter being for God's decision alone. Even on his death-
bed, when lamenting the state of the realm and calling Richard the
landlord and not the king of England, he never preaches rebellion.
And he mentions deposition only in the sense that Richard by his own
conduct is deposing himself. York utters the most correct sentiments.
Like the Bastard he is for supporting the existing government. And
though he changes allegiance he is never for rebellion. As stated above,
the gardener was against the deposition of Richard.

As well as being a study of medievalism, Richard takes his place
among Shakespeare's many studies of the kingly nature. He is a king
by unquestioned title and by his external graces alone. But others have
written so well on Richard's character that I need say no more.

Lastly, for political motives, there is the old Morality theme of
Respublica. One of Shakespeare's debts in *Richard II* is to *Woodstock*;
and this play is constructed very plainly on the Morality pattern, with
the king's three uncles led by Woodstock inducing him to virtue, and
Tressilian Bushy and Green to vice. There are traces of this motive in
Shakespeare's play, but with Woodstock dead before the action begins
and Gaunt dying early in it the balance of good and evil influences is
destroyed. Bushy, Green and Bagot, however, remain very plainly
Morality figures and were probably marked in some way by their dress
as abstract vices. If Shakespeare really confused Bagot with the Earl
of Wiltshire (according to a conjecture of Dover Wilson) he need not
be following an old play heedlessly: he would in any case look on them
all as a gang of bad characters, far more important as a gang than as
individuals, hence not worth being careful over separately. Once again,
as in the earlier tetralogy, England herself, and not the protagonist,
is the main concern. Gaunt speaks her praises, the gardener in describing his own symbolic garden has her in mind. As part of the great cycle
of English history covered by Hall's chronicle the events of the reign
of Richard II take their proper place. But here something fresh has
happened. The early tetralogy had as its concern the fortunes of England in that exciting and instructive stretch of her history. *Richard II*
has this concern too, but it also deals with England herself, the nature
and not merely the fortunes of England. In *Richard II* it is the old
brilliant medieval England of the last Plantagenet in the authentic
succession; in *Henry IV* it will be the England not of the Middle Ages
but of Shakespeare himself. We can now see how the epic comes in
and how *Richard II* contributes to an epic effect. Those works which
we honour by the epic title always, among other things, express the
feelings or the habits of a large group of men, often of a nation. However centrally human, however powerful, a work may be, we shall not
give it the epic title for these qualities alone. It is not the parting of

Hector and Andromache or the ransoming of Hector's body that make the *Iliad* an epic; it is that the *Iliad* expresses a whole way of life. Shakespeare, it seems, as well as exploiting the most central human affairs, as he was to do in his tragedies, was also impelled to fulfil through the drama that peculiarly epic function which is usually fulfilled through the narrative. Inspired partly perhaps by the example of Daniel and certainly by his own genius, he combined with the grim didactic exposition of the fortunes of England during her terrible ordeal of civil war his epic version of what England was.

This new turn given to the History Play is a great stroke of Shakespeare's genius. Through it he goes beyond anything in Hall or Daniel or even Spenser. Hall and Daniel see English history in a solemn and moral light and they are impressive writers. Spenser is a great philosophical poet and epitomises the ethos of the Elizabethan age. But none of these can truly picture England. . . .

Of this great new epic attempt *Richard II* is only the prelude. What of England it pictures is not only antique but partial: the confined world of a medieval courtly class. In his next plays Shakespeare was to picture (with much else) the whole land, as he knew it, in his own day, with its multifarious layers of society and manners of living.

The Political Problem in Shakespeare's
Lancastrian Tetralogy

by Irving Ribner

Any discussion of Shakespeare's history plays must begin with the awareness that they are, before all else, works of imaginative literature. But, as Lily B. Campbell has shown, Shakespeare in writing them was not only a dramatist, but a historian as well, assuming and fulfilling the function of the historian as the Elizabethans saw it.[1] The plays are thus important social documents, and they must also be studied as such, for their historical and political content did much to determine their content as drama. Although much progress in the study of the political content of the plays has been made by recent works of scholarship,[2] one very vital question does not seem to me yet to have been adequately answered, and it is the question upon which any interpretation of Shakespeare's political philosophy must ultimately depend. That is the precise political position taken by Shakespeare in the conflict between Richard II and Henry Bolingbroke. I do not believe we can agree with Dover Wilson that "he takes sides neither with Richard nor Bolingbroke."[3]

We cannot overstress his "negative capability" which, as a dramatist, enabled Shakespeare to see all sides of complex human situations, and we cannot deny that his primary interest in the protagonists was as men and not as symbols of political principles. But as a historian, he saw in the conflict between Richard and Bolingbroke a crucial political problem of his age. When we consider the moral and didactic functions which Elizabethans always made history serve, it is incon-

"The Political Problem in Shakespeare's Lancastrian Tetralogy" by Irving Ribner. From Studies in Philology, *49 (1952), 171–184. Copyright © 1952 by the University of North Carolina Press. Reprinted by permission of the publisher.*

[1] *Shakespeare's "Histories" Mirrors of Elizabethan Policy* (San Marino, 1947), *passim.* . . .

[2] Campbell, and E. M. W. Tillyard, *Shakespeare's History Plays* (New York, 1947) are perhaps the most thorough and illuminating which have thus far appeared.

[3] Introduction to his New Cambridge Edition of *Richard II* (Cambridge, 1939), p. xxxv.

ceivable that he could have been entirely neutral. For Richard and
Henry as men, Shakespeare the dramatist has an all embracing human
sympathy, but on the political issues involved in their struggle, Shakespeare the historian could not be impartial. I propose here to treat the
plays of the Lancastrian tetralogy entirely from the point of view of
their political content and to arrive at some estimation of Shakespeare's
political position.

Tillyard and Campbell have examined the Tudor chronicles as well
as contemporary literary works of history such as the *Mirror for
Magistrates,* and they have demonstrated that Elizabethans saw history
from Richard II to Henry VII in a conventional pattern which was
stated and perpetuated by apologists for the Tudor regime. This pattern saw the deposition of Richard II as the great crime which had
resulted in the Wars of the Roses and the long years of civil disturbance which only the accession of the Tudors in 1485 had been able
to bring to an end. This is the attitude reflected in the Chronicles
from Polydore Vergil to Holinshed.[4] The crown policy of Tudor England, moreover, held that no matter how great a tyrant a king might
be, he remained the agent of God on earth, and only God had power
to depose him. Rebellion, no matter what the cause, was the greatest
of all possible sins. A healthful society must observe "degree and
order" just as the heavens observed it, with every citizen keeping his
proper place and exercising his proper function in the social hierarchy.
The deposition and murder of Richard II served as the classic example
of how God's judgment would plague a people for a century when
order was disturbed. There can be no doubt that Shakespeare believed
in this almost universally accepted doctrine of degree, and that he
accepted the Tudor doctrines of absolutism and passive obedience.
Too great a concentration upon these traditional ideas and emphases,
however, and too great an attempt to see Shakespeare's history plays
in the light of them, have tended to obscure other elements in the
plays. The Lancastrian plays do not always echo traditional Tudor
doctrine. There are, in fact, other problems raised in Shakespeare's
second tetralogy. It is with these that this paper is concerned.

If, for instance, the Elizabethan audience, as is commonly supposed,
saw in the deposition of Richard only a scene of sacrilege destined to
bring a hundred years of chaos to England, it is difficult to believe that
the followers of Essex would have called for the staging of the play
on the eve of the ill-fated rebellion in 1601, as we know that they did.
If Shakespeare's central purpose was to display the great crime for

---

[4] See Tillyard, particularly pp. 29–54. Indeed one of the great functions of the
chronicles was to support the Tudor doctrines of absolutism and passive obedience
by illustrating the evils of rebellion. . . .

which, according to Polydore Vergil and his followers, the English people suffered God's vengeance until the coming of Henry VII, it is difficult to see why the deposition scene was probably never staged before Elizabeth and was deleted from the quartos of 1597 and 1598. Professor Campbell's conclusion that Shakespeare in *Richard II*, "set forth the political ethics of the Tudors in regard to the rights and duties of a king," [5] seems to be somewhat of an oversimplification. Elizabethans must have perceived in the play at least some doctrine that was not entirely orthodox.[6]

Is it not possible that when Shakespeare began his second tetralogy in 1595 he was not immediately concerned with the problems of "degree" and passive obedience, and that he saw in the deposition of Richard II much more than the commonplace moral lesson which the Tudor political apologists saw in it? Might he not have seen in the conflict between Richard and Bolingbroke other problems, problems which were perhaps more pertinent to the year in which the play was written? I believe that Shakespeare accepted the deposition of Richard as a historical *fait accompli* which—although it ultimately resulted in the Wars of the Roses, to which, following Holinshed closely, he has the Bishop of Carlisle make reference in traditional terms—in its immediate effects was good for England. It is with this good that the plays from *Richard II* to *Henry V* are concerned.

In his attempt to see Shakespeare's history plays within the conventional Tudor pattern, Tillyard tends, in effect, to regard the plays as a continuous pageant beginning with *Richard II* and ending with *Richard III*. At the beginning prosperity is destroyed by the deposition of Richard II, and God's curse falls upon England; then follow the conscience-stricken Henry IV's attempts to preserve his realm, the brief victory of Henry V, followed by the endless rebellions of the *Henry VI* plays which culminate in the enormities of *Richard III*. And then, at

---

[5] Campbell, p. 212.

[6] Evelyn May Albright, who sees Shakespeare as perhaps sympathetic to the aspirations of the Earl of Essex (as we know that his patron, Southampton, was), has held that one of Shakespeare's sources was a manuscript of John Hayward's *Henry IV*, a work which glorified the Lancastrian usurper and argued that a subject's duty was not to the ruler, but to the welfare of the state; after its dedication to the Earl of Essex in 1599 this work resulted in the author's trial and imprisonment. Cf. "Shakespeare's *Richard II* and the the Essex conspiracy," *PMLA*, XLII (1927), 686–720; "Shakespeare's *Richard II*, Hayward's History of Henry IV and the Essex Conspiracy," *PMLA*, XLVI (1931), 694–719. . . . Although most of Miss Albright's thesis has not won general acceptance, she is certainly right in her contention that Shakespeare's Bolingbroke is an affable, courteous and popular hero. Shakespeare is far more sympathetic to him than are any of the chronicle writers, and this is true also of Hayward. Shakespeare's relation to the Essex rebellion remains a puzzling problem which has yet to be satisfactorily settled.

the end of the cycle, appears Henry of Richmond, God's curse is removed and order is restored.[7] This is undoubtedly the course of events which the Tudor chronicles depicted and the emphasis which the chronicles gave them. But what scholars who would emphasize Shakespeare's close adherence to this traditional view—who would regard *Richard II* and its followers as written to fill in events needed to complete the earlier historical series—tend to ignore is that Shakespeare's histories are not one cycle. They are two cycles, written at different times, in different ways, and reflecting two different periods of artistic and intellectual maturity. The cycle of plays which begins with the deposition of Richard II does not culminate in the bloody tyranny of Richard III; it culminates in the glorious victories of Henry V. Out of Richard's deposition proceeds not the cruelest of England's tyrants, but the greatest of English kings.

The earlier cycle, completed by 1592, is thoroughly orthodox and conforms closely to the interpretation of earlier history which we find in Halle.[8] Is it likely that there was any shift in popular political concerns between the time of these plays and 1595 the year in which most scholars agree *Richard II* was written? It is certainly true that the defeat of the Spanish armada in 1588 and the disappearance of Spain as a threat to English security had started a gradual lessening of the fear of internal rebellion which had been so strong in England since Henry VIII's break with the Church of Rome. For Spain was the country to which English Catholics, eager to obey the papal edict that Elizabeth be unseated in favor of a Catholic monarch, might look for support. It is reasonable to speculate that in the years after 1588 and particularly after 1590 when fears of a second armada failed to materialize, as fear of Catholic insurrection began progressively to lessen, the need to exhort the populace from the pulpit and the stage on the evils of rebellion and the holiness of passive obedience began correspondingly to wane.[9] By 1595 another problem had probably begun

[7] Professor Campbell, who does not treat the Henry VI plays because of her uncertainty of their authorship, nevertheless treats the Lancastrian plays as part of a general pattern which requires the events of those earlier plays for its completion. For Professor Campbell, the Tudor pattern presented history as a series of crimes, each of which is followed by God's retribution in the third generation. Thus Richard II was punished for the crime of his grandfather, Edward III; Henry VI was punished for the crime of his grandfather, Henry IV etc. Cf. particularly p. 122.

[8] We should not expect this to be otherwise. There is a little reason to believe that Shakespeare, still young and in his most imitative period, might wish at this time to look too critically at the established and commonplace notions with which he found his sources to abound.

[9] Professor Campbell, who regards the political philosophy of the *Henry IV* plays merely as a restatement of the Tudor doctrine of passive obedience, would see in the rebellion of the Percies a specific representation of the Northern rebellion of 1569. It is difficult to believe that in 1597 and 1598 Shakespeare would care to illus-

to loom increasingly more large as it became evident that Elizabeth would have no heirs, and that was the problem of the succession. Is it not more likely that Shakespeare wrote his Lancastrian tetralogy to delineate the kind of king who must succeed Elizabeth than to show the evil results of rebellion? Although he never condoned the crime of Richard's deposition, the plays do represent a glorification of the deposer and his son. In Richard and Bolingbroke Shakespeare saw two directly antithetical royal types, and by objectively comparing them he could formulate his notion of what a king should and should not be. In the fall of Richard, Shakespeare depicts how a bad king may bring destruction to his country, and in the triumph of the house of Lancaster he shows how similar destruction may be prevented.

What Shakespeare and his contemporaries probably feared most in the years immediately following 1594 was the accession of a weak king, one incapable of maintaining order, under whose reign powerful noble factions would again create chaos in England. This was not a new fear; it had been repeated many times in earlier political writings, but the imminence of Elizabeth's death began, as the 16th century drew to a close, to focus more attention upon the problem. William Tyndale in 1528 had written words which immediately call to mind the conflict between Richard II and Henry Bolingbroke:

> Yea, and it is better to have a tyrant unto thy king: than a shadow; a passive king that doth nought himself, but suffereth others to do with him what they will and to lead him whither they list. For a tyrant, though he do wrong unto the good, yet he punisheth the evil, and maketh all men obey, neither suffereth any man to poll but himself only. A king that is as soft as silk and effeminate, that is to say, turned into the nature of a woman—what with his own lusts, which are the longing of a woman with child, so that he cannot resist them, and what with the wily tyranny of them that ever rule him—shall be much more grievous unto the realm than a right tyrant. Read the chronicles and thou shalt ever find it so.[10]

So wrote one of the fathers of the English Reformation and one of the earliest and most forceful proponents of the doctrines of Tudor absolutism. In *Richard II* Shakespeare presents just such a weak and effeminate king as Tyndale describes, and his answer is much like Tyndale's: better a strong and efficient king with illegal title than such a man.

---

trate a commonplace political philosophy by allusion to a thirty year old rebellion when there were about him political problems of so much more immediate concern. See Campbell, p. 230 ff.

[10] *The Obedience of a Christian Man* (1528), ed. Richard Lovett (London, 1885), pp. 93–4.

Richard II is the last of a long line of British kings of undisputed title. As a man he wins the sympathy of the audience, but as a king he is a failure. Like the King Basilius of Sidney's *Arcadia* he is not lacking in private virtues, but he is utterly without the public virtues which make for efficient rule. The Elizabethans made much of the distinction between private and public virtues.[11] A good private gentleman must have the former; a good king must combine both, as does Sidney's King Euarchus, and in so far as the welfare of his people was concerned, the public virtues were of greater importance. Machiavelli went so far as to deny the relevance of private virtues to the problems of government, and the influence of Machiavelli in Elizabethan thought can no longer be underestimated.

Antithetical to Richard in every respect is Henry Bolingbroke. Indeed, as many critics have pointed out, the entire play is constructed upon the dramatic contrast afforded by these two men. Although Bolingbroke wins little personal sympathy from the audience and his private virtues are questionable, the public virtues which will enable him to remedy the insufficiencies of Richard's reign are evident from his first appearance. Tillyard has suggested that the two characters are symbols of two opposing ways of life, with Richard, as the last of the Plantagenet kings, epitomizing the dying medieval world, and Bolingbroke representing a new way of life opposed to it.[12] Although there may be something anachronistic in Tillyard's attributing to Shakespeare a modern conception of the Middle Ages, there is still truth in his observation.[13] The contrast between Richard and Bolingbroke, moreover, is not only one of character, but one of action as well. Within the scope of *Richard II*, Shakespeare has Bolingbroke confronted with each of the two problems which had confronted Richard and had led to his disaster: the quarrel between Mowbray and Bolingbroke and Bolingbroke's insurrection.

Prefixed to the great deposition scene in the fourth act is a passage of great significance. Just as Bolingbroke had earlier in the play accused Mowbray of complicity in the death of Gloucester, now Bagot

---

[11] See Spenser's letter to Raleigh prefixed to the 1590 *Faerie Queene*. The distinction ultimately goes back to Aristotle. Professor Campbell holds that in this distinction is the essential difference between the history play and tragedy (p. 16).

[12] Tillyard, p. 224 ff.

[13] Hiram Haydn has further described two conflicting world views in Renaissance England, a Christian idealism carried on from the Middle Ages and a new skeptical materialism (which he calls the Counter-Renaissance) made popular by Bruno, Montaigne and Machiavelli, and he has indicated Shakespeare's awareness of these conflicting philosophies and his use of their conflict for dramatic purposes. Cf. *The Counter Renaissance* (New York, 1950), particularly p. 651 ff. In the conflict between Richard and Bolingbroke it is possible to see an epitome, to some extent, of these opposing forces.

confronts Aumerle with the same charge, and challenges are thrown down on either side.[14] Richard's inability to handle just such a conflict between powerful nobles had been one of the causes of his downfall. Bolingbroke, however, is complete master of the situation. This scene, writes John Palmer, "was clearly designed to show that Bolingbroke has the political tact and resolution in which Richard has proved so grievously deficient." [15]

The second parallel of action occurs in the abortive insurrection of Aumerle in the fifth act.[16] This scene, which most critics have called extraneous and which is almost always omitted on the stage, is actually an essential part of the dramatic structure. Bolingbroke is here faced with an uprising carried on in the name of the deposed king, who incidentally still lives, and in Elizabethan eyes would be the rightful king in whose name rebellion against a usurper would be justified.[17] That insurrection is not approved by Shakespeare. To York it is a crime against England which even strong paternal feeling cannot permit him to condone, and with his aid this insurrection is summarily put down by the new king. In this deliberate contrast of failure with success, the destruction of the state and its preservation, we have the answer to Shakespeare the historian's political position in the play. He is clearly on the side of Bolingbroke. His type of rule would mean justice and mercy (note his pardon of Aumerle) and the preservation of civil order in England.

How could Shakespeare portray the ineffectiveness of Richard as a king and justify his succession by Bolingbroke without seeming an advocate of rebellion? This is a problem with which the dramatist must have coped. It is possible that in his attempt to solve this problem, rather than in an attempt to outdo Marlowe as is commonly supposed, Shakespeare discovered tragedy of character. For he made Richard the author of his own downfall. Richard is not portrayed as the royal martyr the Tudor chronicles had made of him.[18] Richard destroys and deposes himself, and Bolingbroke by virtue of his abilities,

[14] IV. i. 1–106. All Shakespeare references are to *The Complete Works of William Shakespeare*, ed. G. L. Kittredge (Boston, 1936).

[15] *Political Characters of Shakespeare* (London, 1945), p. 160.

[16] V. ii. 46 ff.

[17] Tillyard, in his discussion of Tudor political doctrine as illustrated by the *Mirror for Magistrates*, states an exception which Elizabethans made to the divine injunction against rebellion: "If the rightful king had been deposed it was lawful to rise against his usurper and reinstate him" (p. 86). Further, he says, "there is never any doubt that Henry IV, the first Lancastrian king was a usurper" (p. 87).

[18] In the anonymous *Woodstock* play with which Shakespeare was unquestionably familiar, and from which he took many suggestions, Richard II is pictured as a petty tyrant, with none of the redeeming qualities with which Shakespeare endows him.

and because he is fortune's minion mounting the wheel in spite of himself,[19] steps into his place. The element of armed rebellion against a lawful king, although it certainly is present in the play, is softened and minimized by the dramatist; dramatically Richard's deposition emerges as the result of his own character, rather than the antagonism of Bolingbroke. King Henry IV, in one of his most famous speeches, and one clearly designed for the information of the audience, tells how kingship was thrust upon him by the necessity of the times:

> Though then, God knows, I had no such intent,
> But that necessity so bow'd the state
> That I and greatness were compelled to kiss.[20]

Richard's downfall was the inevitable result of his own conduct. This is one of the political lessons of the play.

It must be remembered that Richard is not only himself a lawful king, but also a symbol of the Tudor doctrine of kingship. Many critics have pointed out that the most often recurring poetic image in the play is the comparison of Richard to the sun.[21] This is a traditional comparison which illustrates how completely Richard was thought of in terms of Elizabethan political theory. Just as the sun ruled the heavens, its counterpart on earth, the king, ruled the body politic. Richard, moreover, repeats the basic doctrines of Tudor absolutism probably more accurately and more often than does any other character in Elizabethan drama. He offers them as justification for his deeds and calls upon them for protection against his enemies.

A perfect illustration is furnished by the great scene in the third act of *Richard II* when the king returns from Ireland and learns that Bolingbroke is in arms against him. Carlisle and Aumerle urge him to summon up his strength and take action against his enemies, for God will side with a lawful king:

> Fear not, my lord. The Power that made you king
> Hath power to keep you king in spite of all.
> The means that heaven yields must be embrac'd,
> And not neglected; else, if heaven would,
> And we will not, heaven's offer we refuse,
> The proffered means of succour and redress.[22]

God will aid the lawful king who helps himself. But Richard will not

---

[19] See Wilson, pp. xix-xxii and Raymond Chapman, "The Wheel of Fortune in Shakespeare's History Plays," *RES*, I n. s. (1950), 1–7.

[20] *Henry IV, Part 2*, III. i. 72–4.

[21] See, for instance, Samuel Kliger, "The Sun Imagery in *Richard II*," *SP*, XLIV (1948), 196–202.

[22] *Richard II*, III. ii. 27–32.

assert his power; the sole protection he calls upon is the divinity of his kingship:

> Not all the water in the rough rude sea
> Can wash the balm off from an anointed king.
> The breath of worldly men cannot depose
> The deputy elected by the Lord.
> For every man that Bolingbroke hath press'd
> To lift shrewd steel against our golden crown,
> God for his Richard hath in heavenly pay
> A glorious angel. Then, if angels fight,
> Weak men must fall; for heaven still guards the right.[23]

There is a pathetic irony in Richard's proclaiming the commonplaces of Tudor political theory at the very moment when Bolingbroke is making head against him in spite of them. The proclamation of the divinity which guards a king could not carry much conviction to an audience hearing in it the futile remonstrances of a king whose cause it knows is lost. The dramatic impact of the entire scene is not a triumphant statement of the great truths of the Tudors. If anything, the scene illustrates the pathetic insufficiency of these doctrines by themselves. And as the full weight of Richard's situation becomes clear to him in the reports of Salisbury and Scroop, Richard himself abandons hope in the protection of his divine kingship:

> Throw away respect,
> Tradition, form and ceremonious duty;
> For you have but mistook me all this while.
> I live with bread like you, feel want, taste grief,
> Need friends. Subjected thus,
> How can you say to me I am a king? [24]

The notion which had been proclaimed so proudly in the opening lines of the scene has been abandoned and defeated by Richard's final speech:

> He does me double wrong
> That wounds me with the flatteries of his tongue.
> Discharge my followers. Let them hence away,
> From Richard's night to Bolingbroke's fair day.[25]

The orthodox expression of Tudor doctrine in the lines of the scene could not have offended the Elizabethan censor. They apparently

---

[23] III. ii. 54–62.
[24] III. ii. 172–7.
[25] III. ii. 215–18.

blinded him to the dramatic impact of the scene as a whole which
certainly does not lend support to the doctrines so dear to Elizabeth
and her council. It is interesting that Elizabeth never overcame her
intense dislike for the play, although Sir William Cecil apparently
had no objection to it.[26] Perhaps the queen's dramatic perception was
keener than that of her chief minister.

The play thus illustrates the failure of a weak king, depending only
upon his divine protection and God's injunction against rebellion, to
prevent civil disturbance raised by powerful noble factions. In the
Henry IV plays Shakespeare shows us an unlawful king, one who in
Elizabethan eyes would not have the protection of hereditary right,
faced with precisely the same problem that had faced Richard in the
preceding play. But Henry has the public virtues which Richard lacks,
and these make him successful in spite of the illegality of his title.

In the final acts of *Richard II,* Shakespeare had already contrasted
Richard and Bolingbroke by two significant parallels of action. In the
Henry IV plays he continues this deliberate contrast on a larger scale.
It is significant that Shakespeare chose to build his plays around the
rebellion of the Percies. Here we have again a powerful noble faction
creating civil disturbance in an effort to unseat the king. But the king
this time is a technically unlawful king and Mortimer, the new claim-
ant, has hereditary right to bolster him, for he is Richard's legally
designated heir. Here we have the precise situation of Aumerle's rebellion again, but this time in a force and scope larger than anything
of which Aumerle and his friends were capable. The problem is again
brought sharply into focus: which is more important, the divine sanction of hereditary right, or proven ability to govern. The parallel
between *Richard II* and *Henry IV, Part 1* is perfectly expressed in
King Henry's speech to Prince Hal:

> For all the world,
> As thou art to this hour, was Richard then
> When I from France set foot at Ravenspurgh;
> And even as I was then is Percy now.[27]

The rebellion against Henry IV, as Shakespeare repeats throughout
both plays, is carried on in the name of Richard II. Northumberland
and his followers, if only for expediency, nevertheless identify themselves with the cause of the dead king. The uprising of the Archbishop
of York is thus described:

> But now the Bishop
> Turns insurrection to religion.

[26] Wilson, p. xxxii.
[27] *Henry IV, Part 1,* III. ii. 93–6.

> Supposed sincere, and holy in his thoughts,
> He's follow'd both with body and with mind;
> And doth enlarge his rising with the blood
> Of fair King Richard, scrap'd from Pomfret stones;
> Derives from heaven his quarrel and his cause.[28]

It is a holy war, waged in the name of the injured agent of God. If Shakespeare, in *Richard II*, had favored the cause of the deposed king, it is difficult to believe that he could be so inconsistent as to deliberately select for condemnation in the following plays uprisings specifically carried on in the dead king's cause. And condemn them he does, in unmistakable terms, even condoning the shameful perfidy of Prince John of Lancaster because it is directed against rebel forces.[29] Shakespeare was interested in condemning civil disorder, no matter in what cause it were raised.

The audience is never allowed to forget "by what by-paths and indirect crook'd ways" Bolingbroke attained his crown. Shakespeare does not absolve him from the guilt of Richard's murder, and he never has the opportunity to expiate his sin by his long contemplated pilgrimage to the holy land. Henry V feels also the weight of this sin, and he expresses it in his prayer before Agincourt.[30] It is a sin which colors all of Bolingbroke's life and which denies him the rest that should follow his victories. But his reign, it must be emphasized, is not therefor condemned. It has manifestly succeeded where Richard's had failed, and Henry's success in maintaining order goes far to compensate for the illegality of his title. When the king, in his famous deathbed speech[31] tells of his usurpation, Prince Hal in reply speaks words that sum up the author's political position:

> My glorious liege,
> You won it, wore it, kept it, gave it me;
> Then plain and right must my possession be:
> Which I with more than with a common pain
> 'Gainst all the world will rightfully maintain.[32]

[28] *Henry IV, Part 2*, I. i. 200–206.
[29] *Ibid.*, IV. ii.
[30]
> Not to-day, O Lord,
> O, not to-day, think not upon the fault
> My father made in compassing the crown!
> I Richard's body have interred new;
> And on it have bestowed more contrite tears
> Than from it issued forced drops of blood.
>   *Henry V*, IV. i. 309–14.

[31] *Henry IV, Part 2*, IV. v. 178–220.
[32] IV. v. 221–5.

In Bolingbroke's ability to hold his throne and promote the good of England lies the right of his son to rule as England's greatest king.

Although dramatically each of the *Henry IV* plays must stand as an independent structure,[33] one theme does run through both plays, and that is the shaping of the ideal king who will rule as Henry V. The qualities which make him "the mirror of all Christian kings" have been amply commented upon. The thing to be noted here is that they include, in large measure, the public virtues so firmly etched in the portrait of his father. It is significant also that very early in *Henry V*, in the rebellion of Richard, Earl of Cambridge, Henry V faces the same test his father had faced. This rebellion he subdues as efficiently as Bolingbroke had subdued those of Aumerle and the Percies. Henry V is the direct product of his father's usurpation and reign. Shakespeare in his next play goes on to exhibit with the full force of his eulogy the ultimate result of Bolingbroke's accession to the throne of England. "The king (Henry IV) and with him England, has won. The wild young prince has developed qualities which will make him the greatest of English kings." [34]

It must thus be recognized that Shakespeare's Lancastrian plays, when considered as a unit in themselves, as their circumstances of composition make it necessary that they be considered, illustrate something more than the traditional Tudor interpretation of earlier history. Indeed Shakespeare never contented himself with the mere commonplace of his age. He accepted the doctrines of absolutism and passive obedience, but the plays are not mere caveats against rebellion. If he was concerned with any political problem it was with the qualities which make for efficient kingship, and if he was concerned with any immediate political situation, it was that of the type of ruler who should succeed Elizabeth. He believed in the doctrine of degree, but he concluded that if the demands of the divinely sanctioned social hierarchy conflicted with the obvious good of England, the latter must take precedence. When, with this criterion in mind, he compared the reigns of Richard II and Henry IV, he chose the latter, and in doing so he, knowingly or unknowingly, modified the Tudor conception of earlier history. The surest political conviction which emerges from these latter history plays is that the test of a good king is his ability to maintain civil order, and that this ability is ultimately more important than the divine sanction of hereditary right.

[33] See M. A. Shaaber, "The Unity of Henry IV," in *J. Q. Adams Memorial Studies* (Washington, 1948), pp. 217–27.

[34] Hardin Craig, *An Interpretation of Shakespeare* (New York, 1948), p. 160.

Richard II

by Derek Traversi

. . . The play is one which, on a superficial view, it may be easy
to underestimate. The style in which it is written is highly formal and
elaborate: so much so that it may seem at first sight to be lacking in
the vigor of real life. The formality and the elaboration, however,
correspond to an acute and already highly personal reading of historical events. In Shakespeare's very selective treatment of this royal
tragedy, careful study can detect a consistent concern to distinguish
between fiction and truth, or—to put the matter in another way—to
show the downfall of a traditional conception of royalty and its re-
placement by a political force at once more competent, more truly self-
aware, and more precariously built on the foundations of its own
desire for power. The problems, moral and political alike, posed by
this development will provide the starting point, a few years later, for
a series of plays that represent one of the highest points in the dramatist's earlier career.

In accordance with this general purpose the action of *Richard II*
opens on a note of high formality, as the feudal lords Bolingbroke and
Mowbray are uneasily confronted under the eyes of their king. Both
these courtly rivals, presented in the initial act of replacing unity by
strife, allegiance by passionate self-assertion, are still grouped in a
pattern of loyalties dependent upon the crown; but, although they are
at first careful to maintain the appearances of loyal respect, their
formal statements of allegiance are soon replaced by blunt expressions
of mutual defiance.

> *Now,* Thomas Mowbray, do I turn to thee,
> And mark my greeting well;   (I. i)

and as Bolingbroke goes on to deliver his bitter challenge, and receives
the tense, strained rhetoric of his rival's reply, we are made aware that
the formality of the original exchanges is being replaced by something

"Richard II." *From Derek Traversi,* An Approach to Shakespeare, *Vol. I (New
York: Doubleday & Company, Inc., 1969). Copyright © 1969 by Doubleday & Company, Inc. Reprinted by permission of the publisher.*

else, by a mood which includes, among other things, a notable sense of
artifice and strain.

The change of tone is explained at least in part by the nature of the
grievances which separate these rival lords; for these, and their final
relation to the king himself, are something less than transparent. The
main charges in Bolingbroke's indictment are solid enough. They
include the embezzlement of royal revenues for "lewd employments,"
persistent intrigue, and, above all, a part in the plotting of the Duke
of Gloucester's death; the last accusation, most ominously of all, involves the king himself, the center of the feudal structure of loyalty to
which lip service is still being paid, in ambiguity and a suggestion of
guilt. Mowbray's reply, though rhetorically impressive, is notably
evasive in the realm of fact. *Part* of the money received from the royal
treasury was, he admits, held back, but—so it seems—to repay a debt
contracted on another occasion; and whilst denying that Gloucester's
death lies to his charge, he admits to neglect of his "sworn duty" in
that case and confesses, though with affirmations of subsequent repentance and reconciliation, to a plot against the life of Richard's
uncle, John of Gaunt. Whatever the precise facts may be—and they
are left deliberately vague—this is clearly a world more complex than
that of rhetorical defiance and knightly conflict: and in it the king
himself, though maintaining an attitude of royal impartiality, is more
deeply involved than he cares to admit.

Richard's increasing evasiveness, indeed, is a notable feature of these
early scenes. His first interventions in the quarrel are proper statements of detachment:

> Mowbray, impartial are our eyes and ears . . .
> He is our subject, Mowbray; so art thou:
> Free speech and fearless I to thee allow.   (I. i)

So indeed should a king speak and act in the following of his vocation;
but as the accusations implicitly approach his person, there is an increasing sense that this fracas is touching dangerous ground. Almost
imperceptibly, this possibility affects the firmness of the royal stand.
As Mowbray persists in answering defiance with defiance, Richard's
initial gesture of peacemaking takes on a cynical, almost a bored expression:

> Let's purge this choler without letting blood . . .
> Forget, forgive: conclude and be agreed;
> Our doctors say this is no month to bleed.   (I. i)

Is this to be ascribed to intelligence or to indifference, to superior
understanding or to a tendency in the speaker to evade the decisions

and responsibilities to which his office calls him? Perhaps the answer lies finally in the spirit which seems to prevail throughout these early episodes of feudal rivalry. Perhaps the very elaboration of the conflicting expression of defiance points to an underlying void which is filled, on the plane of action, by less respectable motives; and perhaps it is significant that Richard's own regality, which he knows so well how to present in impressive gestures and declarations, can easily turn into a kind of bored indifference which reflects his sense of insecurity. Possibly, indeed, neither the honor which these contending lords so glibly affirm that they value above life nor Richard's own poses of royal impartiality are altogether what they seem to be. In the world of lyrical rhetoric which surrounds the initial court action they are no doubt appropriate, but in the sphere of personal and political responsibility the reality is more obscure, less graciously defined. Richard himself seems to recognize this when, at the end of this first scene, he follows his final assertion of authority—"We were not born to sue, but to command"—with a rueful admission of helplessness: "Which since we cannot do," and only partially covers the lapse by the concluding statement of his purposes: "to make you friends" (I. i).

It is not until after this scene, and the following interrupted tournament, that we see Richard in the company of his favorites, and the presentation of the man begins to prevail over that of the feudal monarch. With Bolingbroke banished and out of mind—as Green puts it: "Well, he is gone; and with him go these thoughts" (I. iv)—a new tone of thriftless cynicism makes itself apparent in the royal comments. The most damaging expression of this is the tone in which he greets the news of John of Gaunt's sickness:

> Now put it, God, in the physician's mind
> To help him to his grave immediately.
>
> (I. iv)

The wish is particularly meaningful because Gaunt, besides being Richard's uncle, represents on his deathbed the traditional spirit of an England associated, for this play, with Edward III and his blood: when Richard desires his death so as to be able to plunder "the lining of his coffers" to provide him with soldiers for the Irish wars, it is in effect his own vocation that he is setting aside. This becomes clear when Richard and Gaunt are directly confronted. Gaunt's famous speech on England (II. i), so easily reduced to a set piece of poetic virtuosity, has a place of its own in the main development. Stylistically, its heightened lyricism is linked to the early court scenes, belongs—like them—to a past which is already succumbing to the inner hollowness that undermines it:

> The setting sun, and music at the close,
> As the last taste of sweets, is sweetest last;
>   (II. i)

the elegiac note so powerful in Gaunt's words anticipates, beyond his
own death, the passing of an order which Richard's authority can no
longer effectively maintain.

Gaunt's poignant references to the past indicate, indeed, death and
loss in the present. His speech is marked further by a Christian tone
which both contrasts with his nephew's present cynicism and anticipates the religious note which Richard's later utterances will associate
with the spectacle of royalty overthrown. As Gaunt's words rise to their
highest intensity in the contemplation of sacred majesty, England
becomes

> this teeming womb of royal kings,
> Fear'd by their breed and famous by their birth,
> Renowned by their deeds as far from home,
> For Christian service and true chivalry,
> As is the sepulchre in stubborn Jewry
> Of the world's ransom, blessed Mary's son.   (II. i)

England, in its state of ideal unity, is an anticipation of perfection—
"This precious stone set in the silver sea"; "This other Eden, demi-
paradise"—and the substance of this blessed state is conveyed through
a sublimation of the chivalry which survives, as a shadow blemished
with strife and egoism, in Richard's own court. The presence of a
Christian aspiration will be balanced, in the king's own later tragic
utterances, by a sense of betrayal, the shadow of the gesture of Judas
which will accompany him through his decline. Meanwhile, we have
"This land of such *dear souls,* this *dear, dear* land" (II. i): beneath this
poignant assertion of patriotism there lies the expression of a tragedy,
reflected in Gaunt's own death, which seeks in the religious reference
a universal expression.

Seen against this background, Gaunt's denunciation of Richard
acquires a deeper meaning. The exchange between them is nicely
balanced between feeling and artifice:

> —I mock my name, great king, to flatter thee:
> —Should dying men flatter with those that live?
> —No, no, men living flatter those that die.
> —Thou, now a-dying, say'st thou flatterest me.
> —O no! thou diest, though I the sicker be.
>   (II. i)

The ideas of flattery and truth, health and sickness, life and death, are interwoven in a way which has relation to the complete conception. Gaunt is dying indeed, and his world with him: but Richard too is set on the path to decline, and his sickness, moreover, is that of his country. Against these realities, the final denunciation put into Gaunt's mouth—"Landlord of England art thou now, not king" (II. i)—is seen in its full meaning. England is described, by contrast with the preceding lyricism, as in a state of sickness; for it has been Richard's crowning irresponsibility to commit his "anointed body," the health of which so closely figures that of his realm, to "those physicians that first wounded thee." The consequences of this betrayal still lie hidden in the future. Meanwhile, Richard's reaction to his uncle's rebuke confirms the moody, contradictory facets of his nature:

> let them die that age and sullens have;
> For both hast thou, and both become the grave.
>   (II. i)

Immediately afterward, however, this bitterness is seen to imply an awareness of his own state and of the baseless fictions of loyalty which surround him. When York tries to turn his anger by affirming that Gaunt speaks out of love for him, and compares that love, with unconscious irony, to that which Bolingbroke still professes, Richard's reply penetrates for a moment to the reality of events to come:

> Right, you say true: as Hereford's love, so his;
> As theirs, so mine; and all be as it is.   (II. i)

This mood of disillusioned fatalism, mingling insight with a touch of self-indulgence, is very close to Richard's nature. To set this incipient tone of tragic bitterness side by side with the childish callousness which prompts him, in the very shadow of his uncle's death, to seize his revenues, is to respond to a character and a situation which are growing in close relationship toward the revelation of their full reality.

These intimations of growing instability in Richard are followed by a notable change in the attitude of those who have so far professed allegiance to him. In York's defense of Bolingbroke's rights, traditional feudal ideas merge into the defense of selfish interests. On the one hand, the claim of lineage, the rights of normal inheritance, are being properly defended by "the last of noble Edward's sons"; on the other, a world of covetousness and mutual distrust is already feeling its way toward the overthrow of legitimate authority. What is in York indecision, a clash of loyalties, is soon seen to involve in others a more direct awareness of threatened interests. After Richard has left, Northumberland adopts a tone which will be associated with his name in the following plays; the king is "not himself," and the envious counsels of his flatterers will translate themselves into acts " 'Gainst us, our lives, our children, and our heirs" (II. i). The true implications of the rivalries with which the play opened are now emerging in their double nature. If the disintegration of loyalty proceeds from the un-worthiness of its royal fountainhead, it is nonetheless in the form of unwarrantable resentment, the maintenance of selfish positions, that it extends itself.

Disintegration, indeed, is the final impression left by this scene with which the first stage of the play draws to a close. In the mounting indignation of the nobility, balanced between patriotic concern and self-interest, we see reflected the breaking unity of the English state. The episode ends, significantly, after Northumberland's remarkable phrase,

> even through the hollow eyes of death
> I spy life peering,   (II. i)

with the announcement of Bolingbroke's return. The action is now embarked upon the course which it will follow to the end of the play. The return of Lancaster, as he will from now on call himself, is simul-taneously a necessity, if the foundations of order are to be restored upon the firm, conscious exercise of authority, and an expression of rebellious selfishness, defeating its own purposes by the perverse na-ture of its claim. The contradiction thus indicated between means and ends, between Lancaster's desires and the manner in which he usurps the crown, will dominate the following history.

From this moment up to the encounter between Richard and his rival the scope of the action narrows to present a clash of personalities. The tragic impotence of the king is balanced by his rival's purposeful advance toward the ends he has proposed to himself. From the moment of his setting foot again in England, Bolingbroke's advance is as cau-tious as it is sure. Potentially useful allies, like the young Harry Percy, he greets with effusive thanks and a tactful indication of recom-pense to come:

> And as my fortune ripens with thy love,
> It shall be still thy true love's recompense;
>   (II. iii)

but to those of his enemies who, like the royal favorites Bushy and Green, fall into his hands, justice is inflexibly administered. In his separation, at such moments, of spiritual and political responsibili-ties—

> Bushy and Green, I will not vex your souls,
> Since presently your souls must part your bodies—
>   (III. i)

Bolingbroke shows himself already the father of the future Henry V;
solicitude in the spiritual order can exist side by side with the firm
execution of justice, but the one must not interfere with the practical
necessities of the other. It is always expedient, moreover, that the
sentence should be publicly justified before it is carried out, and so—

> to wash your blood
> From off my hands, here *in the view of men*
> I will unfold some causes of your deaths.
>
> (III. i)

That in this particular case Henry is an instrument of justice is not
to be doubted; but the anxiety to seek public justification for his
necessary ruthlessness will be passed on by him to his son and may,
on future occasions, find less impeccable causes on which to exercise
itself. For the moment, the firm command—"My lord Northumberland, see them dispatch'd"—is significantly followed by an expedient
gesture of courtesy to Richard's queen ("Take special care my greet-
ings be deliver'd") and by the practical aphorism which brings this
episode to a close: "Awhile to work, and after holiday" (III. i).

It is no accident that the presentation of this firm dedication to the
job in hand should be followed by Richard's return to the scene. He
too has been away, spending in Ireland the resources plundered from
Gaunt, and his return is the occasion for a typical display of senti-
ment, marks the reunion of "a long-parted mother" with the child
who "plays fondly with her tears and smiles in meeting." Richard as
he returns to face his formidable rival at once expresses tragic sentiments and plays with his emotions, "weeping, smiling," as he greets
the earth which both inspires him to genuine love and is used by him
as the occasion for a self-conscious display of emotion. As he goes on,
in the course of the same speech, to compare his enemies to "spiders"
and "heavy-gaited toads," to "stinging nettles" and "lurking adders,"
Richard in effect reduces tragedy to melodrama. Beneath the artifice
and the pathos which are so closely interwoven in what he says, we
may feel the presence of that distraught and essentially morbid, febrile
imagination which is as much part of his nature as the capacity to
respond with an impressive show of tragic dignity to his situation as
a king betrayed. His emotions, indeed, have throughout an unconscious as well as a conscious content; and this gives the character, beyond its conventionality and its public significance, a depth and complexity possibly greater than any so far attained by Shakespeare in
his dramatic development.

These qualities soon reveal themselves in terms of his incapacity
to face practical necessity. Confronted by immediate danger, Richard

is ready enough to take up the conception of the divine vocation which justifies his kingship to assert that

> Not all the water in the rough rude sea
> Can wash the balm from an anointed king;
>   (III. ii)

but it is not long before we are brought to see that this rhetorical confidence is balanced in him only by personal weakness and an intimate disposition to give way to despair. Within five minutes of having thus placed his confidence in God, he is considering, not without a kind of complacency, a certain self-regarding pleasure in the contemplation of disaster, the possible loss of his realm:

> Say, is my kingdom lost? why, 'twas my care;
> And what loss is it to be rid of care? . . .
> Cry woe, destruction, ruin and decay;
> The worst is death, and death will have his day.
>   (III. ii)

The fact is that, personally and politically, Richard is not equipped to cope with his enemies. His best, his most nearly profound utterances, reveal incapacity to act consistently, even a marked tendency to hysterical evasion of the truth. A tragic sentimentalist by nature, though one capable from time to time of rousing himself moodily and dangerously to resentful action, he uses his moments of misfortune to elaborate his woes poetically, even to take a kind of perverse pleasure —actor-like—in expressing his unhappy state.

These outbursts lead finally, in the culminating speech of the scene, to a full expression of despair. As always, a certain conventionality persists in the tone of Richard's lament, but can be felt in the process of giving way to a stronger current of emotion:

> For God's sake, let us sit upon the ground
> And tell sad stories of the death of kings—
> How some have been deposed, some slain in war,
> Some haunted by the ghosts they have deposed,
> Some murder'd by their wives; some sleeping kill'd,
> All murder'd.   (III. ii)

Basically, of course, this famous speech rests on a series of medieval commonplaces, presents a traditional catalogue of the misfortunes that, by the compensating action of Fortune's wheel, accompany the dangerous exaltation of the king. The examples are familiar; but in the flow of the expression, the rise of the voice to the longer period in "Some haunted by the ghosts they have deposed," and the fall to

"All murder'd," we find conveyed, side by side with a true tragic
sense, a notion of the insignificance which haunts the pomp of royalty,
this particular speaker's capacity for dwelling on his own tragedy,
exacting from his plight a sad refinement of sensation. Richard, true
to character, at once expresses his tragedy in terms which genuinely
move us—for it is a true tragedy, and it is an anointed king whom
his subjects, sworn to loyalty, are about to betray—and finds a certain
self-regarding pleasure in the consideration of his unhappy condition;
so that it is not surprising that the speech, after the grave beauty to
which it has risen in the contemplation of the vicissitudes of royalty,
falls away into hysteria and self-pity:

> Cover your heads and mock not flesh and blood
> With solemn reverence. Throw away respect,
> Tradition, form, and ceremonious duty,
> For you have but mistook me all this while.
> I live with bread like you, feel want,
> Taste grief, need friends. Subjected thus,
> How can you say to me I am a king?　　(III. ii)

There is still an appeal here to the traditional sanctions that accompany the royal office, to the "reverence," "form," and "ceremony" that
surround a legitimate king; but it is at the same time an appeal theatrically conceived, a turning of tragedy to self-exhibition which at
once attains, in the broken rhythm of the final lines, a real pathos
and covers a weak man's resentment against what he prefers to regard
as the incomprehensible turns of fate.

Such a man can be no rival for the clear-sighted and ruthless politician who is determined to replace him on the throne. The "brazen
trumpet" of Bolingbroke's messenger conveys "the breath of parley"
into the "ruined ears" of Richard, pitifully sheltered behind the "rude
ribs" of his ancient castle. The forms of loyal service, which the newcomer is at first careful to maintain, conceal the realities of domina-
tion, the "tender show" of "stooping duty" is stressed almost sub-
serviently to cover the bare grasping of power that underlies it. Northumberland, bringing what is in effect his new master's ultimatum,
and disposed to respond to the new situation with a courtier's eye
firmly fixed upon the main chance, covers it with a wealth of stylistic
affectation. Richard, on his side, is perfectly aware of his situation.
It has never been intelligence he has lacked, but something else, less
easily definable but not, for a man placed as he is, less important. We
may, if we will, call this something consistency of character; and its
lack expresses itself, even as he replies with an assumption of weakness, in the awareness that a stern reality is undermining the content
of his words:

> We do debase ourselves, cousin, do we not,
> To look so poorly, and to speak so fair.
>
> (III. iii)

Already, indeed, Richard looks forward to the march of events which, derived in great part from his own weakness, is leading inexorably to a tragic conclusion:

> Oh God, oh God, that e'er this tongue of mine,
> That laid the sentence of dread banishment
> On yon proud man, should take it off again
> With words of sooth! O, that I were as great
> As is my grief, or lesser than my name!
> Or that I could forget what I have been,
> Or not remember what I must be now!
>
> (III. iii)

Here, at least, the utterance is simple, direct enough to pass beyond artifice and pretense to penetrate to the true extent of a royal tragedy.

More often, however, Richard's sense that the reversal of his original judgment will undo him expresses itself in what he knows to be, even as he speaks, "idle talk." This is apparent in the elaborate self-exhibition of "What must the king do now? must he submit?" and the lines which follow:

> I'll give my jewels for a set of beads,
> My gorgeous palace for a hermitage,
> My gay apparel for an almsman's gown,
> My figured goblets for a dish of wood,
> My sceptre for a palmer's walking staff,
> My subjects for a pair of carved saints,
> And my large kingdom for a little grave,
> A little, little grave, an obscure grave;
> Or I'll be buried in the king's highway,
> Some way of common trade, where subject's feet
> May hourly trample on their sovereign's head;
> For on my heart they tread now whilst I live;
> And buried once, why not upon my head?
>
> (III. iii)

In these words, and in the rest of the speech, artifice, weakness, and pathos are variously interwoven. It is interesting to compare this utterance to that, partially similar, which expressed Henry VI's nostalgia for the simple life when faced with the horrors of civil war. The artificial construction is parallel, but is put to ends substantially different; for in Richard, far more than in Henry, it is a kind of pathetic self-pity, as much the exhibition of sorrow as grief itself, that prevails. Sensing that he is doomed, Richard exploits his condition self-consciously; but his artifice, besides being moving as related to a royal tragedy, is sufficiently realized in terms of character to evoke that compassion which only the emotions of a person can give. For Richard, even as he "plays the wanton" with his woes, is aware that just this is what he is doing:

> Would not this ill do well? Well, well, I see
> I talk but idly, and you laugh at me.
> (III. iii)

The speaker's feeling, precisely by being aware of its artificial expression, becomes more real than that of Henry VI, less confined to the literary order and more capable of arousing pity.

The end of this confrontation confirms the situation of its central figures by giving them external projection. Brought back to reality by Northumberland's blunt request, "may it please you to come down," Richard takes up once more the image of the sun of royalty which his rival has applied to him: "Down, down I come, like glistening Phaeton." The image, besides answering to the speaker's characteristically aesthetic self-awareness, leads directly to the meeting with Bolingbroke, in which power, still cloaked in the forms of loyalty, is brought face to face with helplessness, with what Northumberland, typically cruel to the fallen, brushes aside as "the fondness of a frantic man." Henry, kneeling in the external show of deference, calls upon his followers to "show fair duty to his majesty"; but Richard, not content to respond to these empty shows, penetrates more directly to the bare facts of his situation when he says, calling upon his rival to rise:

> Up, cousin, up; your heart is up, I know,
> Thus high at least, although your knee be low.
> (III. iii)

To the newcomer's sober statement, "I come but for mine own," he replies, with a still more penetrating realism, "Your own is yours, and I am yours, and all," and follows this, most realistically of all, with his rejoinder to Bolingbroke's empty offer of service:

> Well you deserve; they well deserve to have,
> That know the strong'st and surest way to get.
> (III. iii)

The distance traveled by Richard since the early scenes of courtly pageantry is never more apparent than at this moment, in which his

personal tragedy is seen as the foundation for a long political development to follow after his death.

From the moment of his spectacular descent "into the base court,"
Richard's fate is to all intents and purposes sealed. The latter part of
the play confirms his fall and consummates the process of his rival's
rise to power. The proclamation of Bolingbroke as king is followed
by the demand, pitilessly pressed, that his predecessor should publicly
renounce his office: "Are you contented to resign the crown?" (IV. i).
In Richard's reply, complex and contradictory by comparison with
this ruthless challenge, the germ of many later Shakespearean developments can be discerned. His thoughts turn, not merely on natural
grief, but on a sense of vanity—*nothingness*—which the very artificiality of the expression paradoxically deepens:

> Ay, no; no, ay; for I must nothing be; . . .
> Make me, that *nothing* have, with *nothing* grieved,
> And thou with all pleased, that hast all achieved!
> Long mayst thou live in Richard's seat to sit,
> And soon lie Richard in an earthy pit!   (IV. i)

We must feel at this moment that the word nearest to the speaker's
heart is, after all his elaborations, *nothing*, and that his mood issues
in an intense craving for the release from effort and choice which
only death can bring. But the *nothingness*, it must be added, is also
reflected in Bolingbroke's absorbing pursuit of power. Richard's attitude to his political responsibilities is of course extreme, one more
example of his essential self-indulgence; but his comment at this decisive moment in his fortunes is also relevant for the usurper who
is now, with little but devices of policy in his mind, preparing to replace him on the throne. *Nothing, nothing*: in the long run any
relevant conception of political power will have to come to terms
with the challenge which that word implies and which so much of the
public behavior shown in this play amply confirms.

Meanwhile, however, the case against Richard is bitterly pressed
home. To his final, exhausted question, "What more remains?" there
corresponds, not any expression of human compassion on the part of
his enemies, but the prosecution of the accusations prepared against
him:

> No more, but that you read
> These accusations and these grievous crimes,
>   (IV. i)

followed by an admission that the real purpose of this proceeding
is to justify the usurper in the eyes of the world. Surrounded by so

much ruthless calculation, Richard's very real weaknesses become increasingly subsidiary to the pathos of his tragedy as king deposed. His reply to Northumberland raises to a fresh level of poignancy the Christian parallel which runs as a principal thread of feeling through the tragedy:

> Nay, all of you that stand and look upon,
> Whilst that my wretchedness doth bait myself,
> Though some of you with Pilate wash your hands
> Showing an outward pity; yet you Pilates
> Have here deliver'd me to my sour cross,
> And water cannot wash away your sin.   (IV. i)

Our reaction to this is necessarily double. Richard is engaged to the last in exhibiting his emotions, playing with feelings the seriousness of which we cannot, in the light of his known failings and consequent responsibility for his state, fully accept; and yet the betrayal, based on the calculation that everywhere surrounds him, implies a setting aside of every normal human obligation, and its effect is deepened by the fact that it is a king whom his subjects, sworn to loyalty, are engaged in deserting. It is the tragedy of betrayal, as well as that of fallen royalty, that is being enacted round Richard's isolated and unhappy person; and the treachery, moreover, is doubly personal, insomuch as Richard has, by his own past behavior and dubious choices, betrayed himself before he was in turn betrayed:

> Nay, if I turn mine eyes upon myself,
> I find myself a traitor with the rest.
>   (IV. i)

Richard has betrayed the office which he has held unworthily, and the betrayal has bred a corresponding treachery which leads to his destruction. Bolingbroke, in a way not finally dissimilar, will prove in due course to be divided between the political virtues that are undoubtedly his and a desire for power which is ominously reflected in the court of time-serving and ambitious lords who seek their own convenience by accompanying his rise to authority.

Beneath the conventionality of Richard's expression lies, indeed, an effort to define his relation to the tragic course of events. This culminates in his request for a mirror, in which once more artificiality, conscious self-exhibition, and a measure of true self-exploration are variously blended. Henry, now secure master of the situation, contemptuously accedes to the latest emotional trick of his victim, whilst Northumberland, ruthless as ever, presses the charges against him—

> Read o'er this paper while the glass doth come—

and stresses yet again the political motive beneath his disapproval of his master's careless concession:

> The commons will not then be satisfied.
>
> (IV. i)

When the mirror is at last brought, Richard contemplates his features in it with a kind of tragic self-analysis. This opens, as he breaks the glass, with a typically artificial statement: "How soon my sorrow hath destroy'd my face;" but the comment offered by Bolingbroke points to a deeper contrast between shadow and reality, which is not without tragic content:

> The shadow of your sorrow hath destroy'd
> The shadow of your face.

Bolingbroke perhaps speaks here more deeply than he knows; but the observation produces from Richard, as he takes up the related concepts of "shadow," "sun," and "substance," an indication of the deeper roots of his tragedy:

> Say that again.
> The shadow of my sorrow! ha! let's see!
> 'Tis very true, my grief lies all within;
> And these external manners of laments
> Are merely shadows to the unseen grief
> That swells with silence in the tortured soul;
> There lies the substance.   (IV. i)

One can trace in Shakespeare's work the various stages of a process by which literary artifice, expanding in complexity and psychological correspondence, becomes an instrument of self-analysis. We have already found ample traces of this development in *Romeo and Juliet*; and now the person of Richard, as revealed here, represents a further important stage in the same process. For Richard, as will later be the case for Hamlet, the outer forms of grief are mere "shadows" of the "substance" within; between the tragic content of the two characters there is, of course, no comparison, but a process could be traced by which the artifice of the one is transformed into the greater complexity of the other. Once more, the later plays in the series will throw light on the nature of this transformation. For the moment, Richard's sense of his tragedy leads to the final breakdown, which accompanies his request for "leave to go"

> Whither you will, so I were from your sights,

in which the measureless bitterness of his situation is amply expressed.

By the last scenes of the play, Richard has been awakened in no
uncertain terms from his former "dream" of worldly felicity to "the
truth of what we are":

> A king of beasts indeed; if aught but beasts,
> I had been still a happy king of men;
>
> (V. i)

though we may doubt even now whether, beneath the pathos and
the horror, the speaker has understood how far he is himself con-
nected with the world which he has found such good reason to de-
spise. Everything in the action at this stage—Richard's increasingly
severe imprisonment, the fear which prompts York servilely to accuse
his own son of treason to his new master (V. ii. iii)—confirms this bitter estimate. Richard's last speech, the immediate prelude to his
murder, opens against this somber background of fear and treachery,
with what seems at first sight an academic exercise in poetic pes-
simism:

> I have been studying how I may compare
> This prison where I live unto the world.
>
> (V. v)

An oddly remote occupation, we may be tempted to conclude, for a
king plunged into darkness and solitude, and moreover about to die;
but, apart from the fact that a certain measure of artifice is in character, still answers to this particular king's nature as revealed throughout, the development of his thoughts moves beyond mere artifice to
achieve a more valid tragic effect. As his mediations move to their
climax a deeper effect is attained, a more felt reference to the human
situation touched upon, when Richard returns to the idea of *nothing*
which has been so persistently present as a background, expressed and
implied, to his thoughts:

> whate'er I be,
> Nor I nor any man that but man is
> With *nothing* shall be pleased, till he be eased
> With being *nothing*.   (V. v)

Here, at least, beneath the carefully balanced expression, is a serious
attempt to make words respond to feeling, in something like a tragic
statement about life. Richard feels that what he is about to say is
valid not only for himself, but "for any man that but man is," who
shares the essential limitations of the human state. It is worth noting,
moreover, that this increase in depth is at once followed, most im-
probably in terms of realism, by the playing of "music," in what we

may consider a first dim foreshadowing of one of the mature Shakespearean symbols. The harmony, suitably contradictory in its effects to match the speaker's thoughts—

> how sour sweet music is,
> When time is broke and no proportion kept!—

resolves itself into an attempt at more subtle analysis:

> here have I the daintiness of ear
> To check time broke in a disorder'd string;
> But for the concord of my state and time
> Had not an ear to hear my true time broke.
>   (V. v)

Beneath the artificial balance of the phrasing, the speaker is attempting a valid statement on his condition and the errors which have brought him to it, and in the observation which follows—"I wasted time, and now doth time waste me"—he almost succeeds. Even the elaborate expression has a certain justification in terms of character, as the utterance of one who has habitually *acted* on his royal stage, observed, as it were, his attitudes with an eye to public effect and personal gratification:

> Thus play I in one person many people,
> And none contented.   (V. v)

The devices of this speech, to convince fully, would need to be filled out with a sense of personal commitment to a degree here never quite attained: but, imperfect though it may be, the meditation does foreshadow later developments in the presentation of the tragic hero. Certainly the murder which follows is, by comparison, a pedestrian piece of melodrama. Perhaps Richard's last individual word is spoken in his bitter comment to the Groom on the value of human titles and honors: "The cheapest of us is ten groats too dear" (V. v). This is at once legitimate comment and the confirmation of a character, the evaluation of an inhuman situation and the expression of a king who has always tended to find in an effective show of cynicism a refuge from the collapse of his self-indulgent sentiments.

After the murder, the play ends with a brief and sinister indication of the triumph of the new order. Already, it is becoming clear that Bolingbroke's crime, tacitly admitted as such, will bring neither personal nor political peace. The "latest news" is that the "rebels"—not now his own supporters, but those who have in turn risen against his usurped power—have "consumed with fire" the town of Cicester. On all sides, executions respond to a renewal of civil strife; the heads of numerous "traitors"—so called by he who has just ceased to be such—

are on their way to London, and the spiritual power, henceforth to be increasingly involved in political intrigues, is curtailed by the death of the Abbot of Westminster and the banishment of the loyal and plain-spoken Carlisle. Upon this catalogue of mischance and cross-purposes, the murderers of Richard enter with his body, not to be commended for their "deed of slander," but yet to pin firmly on the real assassin the guilt to which he himself admits. To Exton's unanswerable "From your own mouth, my lord, did I this deed," Henry can only correspond with a statement of moral contradiction, the first of those that will be almost habitual in his mouth:

> They love not poison that do poison need,
> Nor do I thee: though I did wish him dead,
> I hate the murderer, love him murdered.
>
> (V. vi)

Here is the politician, typically engaged in shuffling off the responsibility for his decisions upon others; but beneath the careful balance of the phrasing, the "guilt of conscience" is firmly placed where it belongs, and the new king's last words announce the intention, which will accompany him to his death as an unfulfilled aspiration, to redeem his "guilt" by a spiritual enterprise in the Holy Land. This aspiration, the failure to fulfill it, and its transformation into a more limited national purpose under his son are the themes of the later, greater plays to follow.[1]

---

[1] A more exhaustive account of *Richard II* is given in my book *Shakespeare: From "Richard II" to "Henry V"* (Stanford and London, 1957).

From *Richard II* to *Henry V:*
A Closer View

by Leonard F. Dean

It has been urged in recent years that many of the features and the essential themes of Shakespeare's English history plays were derived from his chronicle sources. This view naturally stresses the considerable amount of popular history in the plays—the patriotic pageantry and spectacle, the orthodox moral and political lessons, the stock characterization of good and bad rulers, wise old counselors and parasitic flatterers. It stresses particularly the theme which is so strong in Hall's Chronicle, the interpretation which asserts that England was happy under Edward III, that Richard II was a weak king, that his deposition by Henry IV was politically necessary and led to a moment of heroic order under Henry V, but that the deposition also brought down God's wrath in the form of the Wars of the Roses, and that peace and divine blessing were restored with the defeat of the bad king Richard III and the subsequent union of Lancaster and York through the marriage of Elizabeth and Henry VII, which founded the Tudor dynasty. J. Dover Wilson sums it up: "Hall furnished the frame and stretched the canvas for the whole Shakespearian cycle, *Richard II* to *Richard III.*" [1]

One difficulty with this stress on Shakespeare's closeness to his chronicle sources is that it tends to reduce him to a Tudor propagandist. But there is more here, insists A. P. Rossiter, than the "moral history of the Lancastrian House . . . and the happy ending in the dawn of Tudarchy." A "pattern is *there,* and it is like Edward Halle's," but "Halle's theory is naive," and Shakespeare cannot be "quite as naive as all that." [2] Another difficulty is that in order to generalize about a pattern (like the Tudor myth) running through

"From Richard II *to* Henry V: *A Closer View"* by Leonard F. Dean. *From Thomas P. Harrison and James H. Sledd, eds.,* Studies in Honor of DeWitt T. Starnes *(Austin: The University of Texas Press, 1967), pp. 37–52 (excerpted). Copyright © 1967 by The University of Texas. Reprinted by permission of the author and publisher.*

[1] Intro. to *King Richard II* (Cambridge, 1939), p. liv.
[2] *Angel With Horns* (New York, 1961), p. 44.

the plays it is necessary to stand so far away that they merge into something known vaguely as the History Play. Only by coming close to the plays can one experience their particular pleasures and learn how a great poet may go beyond the naïvetés of popular history to his own profundities.

When one does come close to *Richard II,* the opening scenes do not sound like the work of a man who knew that he was writing the "first act" of a cycle dramatizing a clear and accepted theory of history. On the contrary, these scenes give the impression of a writer "thinking" his way into his subject. The first scene and its continuation in the third (derived from Hall) are history as spectacle: a royal hearing on charges of treason and a trial by combat; but the necessarily ceremonial language and behavior of spectacle muffle character and theme. The fourth act hints that the real Richard has been play-acting in the spectacular scenes, and that he is therefore bad because he is Machiavellian; but this is not in fact developed to become the key to his character. In the second scene and elsewhere we are told or reminded that Richard is a murderer (of Gloucester) and that he is a bad ruler in the popular sense: addicted to foreign fashions, misled by parasites, guilty of unjust taxation; but again all this is less clear and prominent than it might easily have been. It is perhaps not until Gaunt's great speech on England early in Act II that Shakespeare gives the impression of sensing the true mode and meaning of the play. Gaunt describes England as a fallen world: "This other Eden, demi-paradise . . . is now bound in with shame." The movement is toward the history play as ironic drama: "a vision of what in theology is called the fallen world," where "tragedy's 'this must be' becomes irony's 'this at least is.' " [3] It is a Cold War view of man and the state in which no one is perfect and no one wins. It is opposed to the dreams of popular history (it even implies that happy people have no history) and to its simplifications (professional historians feel that this is Shakespeare's most "truthful" history).

With this in mind one may look back at the confused opening scenes and sense meanings that are only implicit at best. The spectacular ceremonies may illustrate, though imperfectly, a prevailing malaise in which the forms of society are inoperative and disconnected from the realities of power and character. When a country's ruler is himself a murderer, an infected creature of the fallen world rather than the Lord's lieutenant on earth, a fundamental irony exists, and loyal subjects like Gaunt and the widow of Gloucester can only complain helplessly to God. The distance between the ideal pattern and the fallen

[3] Northrop Frye, *Anatomy of Criticism* (Princeton, 1957), p. 285.

fact may be felt behind the dying Gaunt's unrealistic determination
to give "wholesome counsel" to Richard, the "unstaid youth." Counsel
from one generation to another that would be heeded and fruitful in
a more heroic context is irrelevant in this ironic mode, and the
irrelevance is simply underscored by York's well-meant advice: "The
King is come. Deal mildly with his youth;/ For young hot colts being
rag'd do rage the more." Here and elsewhere honest elder statesmen
like York are stultified. He becomes, as he says, a "neuter." His
maxims are turned by circumstances into rootless platitudes. He is so
perplexed as he attempts to deal with the unroyal Richard and the
usurping Bolingbroke that actors have been misled into playing him
as a comic figure. Equally misleading is the attempt to equate him
with the undervalued modern parliamentarian: "The politician who
saves his country by turning his coat is God's most precious gift to a
people which prefers a change of government to a revolution." [4] The
real effect of his role, an appropriate supporting part in ironic drama,
is one of pathetic helplessness. He always, appealingly, wants things
to be better than they can be in the fallen world of this play.

Although by this point in the play (Act II) one may feel that
Shakespeare has begun to sense a viable meaning and tone in his
chaotic material, it is not until Richard's return from Ireland early
in Act III that he finds the best means of developing and dramatizing
his intuitions. The chief means, very simply, are those for which he
became pre-eminent: the dramatic portrayal of character and the expression of theme through the contrast of characters. Starting with
the basic but simple contrast between Richard, an anointed king who
is ruining his country, and Bolingbroke, a treasonous usurper who is
an efficient ruler, Shakespeare first expands and deepens the character of Richard. The psychological features of the portrait were first
persuasively described by Coleridge (in 1813):

> His faults spring entirely from defect of character . . . continually
> increasing energy of thought, and as constantly diminishing power of
> acting. . . . A man with a wantonness in feminine shew, feminine *friend-
> ism,* intensely woman-like love of those immediately about him. . . .
> Constant overflow of feelings; incapability of controlling them; waste of
> that energy which should be reserved for action in the passion and effort
> of resolves and menaces, and the consequent exhaustion. . . . Above all,
> the seeking refuge in despair, so characteristic of inward weakness. . . .
> Exhaustion counterfeiting quiet; and yet the habit of kingliness, the
> effect of flattery from infancy, constantly producing a sort of *wordy* cour-
> age which betrays the inward impotence. The consequent alternation of
> unmanly despair and of ungrounded hope; and throughout the rapid
> transition from one feeling to its opposite.[5]

[4] John Palmer, *Political Characters of Shakespeare* (London, 1948), p. 143.
[5] *Shakespearean Criticism,* ed. T. M. Raysor (Harvard, 1930), I, 148–51.

To this basic outline, Dowden in 1875 added two points which have been often repeated or developed: that Richard is a would-be artist and something of an actor.

> Richard, to whom all things are unreal, has a fine feeling for "situations." Without any of true kingly strength or dignity, he has a fine feeling for the royal situation. . . . Instead of comprehending things as they are, and achieving heroic deeds, he satiates his heart with the grace, the tenderness, the beauty, or the pathos of the situations. Life is to Richard a show, a succession of images; and to put himself into accord with the aesthetic requirements of his position is Richard's first necessity.[6]

The psychological aspect of Richard's character, so acutely analyzed by Coleridge and many others since, is certainly vivid and important. We watch his behavior on the coast of Wales with the knowledge that Bolingbroke's successful invasion has left him with the name of King only, and this ironic circumstance (the title without the reality, the separation of royal symbol and substance) is a proper setting for neurotic display. Clearly Richard, as the physically sick Gaunt had earlier insisted, is the one who is "sick" and plays too nicely with his name. Here and elsewhere, we find ourselves led by the characters around him to respond to his neuroticism in realistically familiar ways: we are by turns ill at ease, embarrassed, ready with sensible advice and admonition, unwillingly tolerant, silently critical and impatient. His language, particularly, is a sign and part of his unbalanced personality. In addition to the extravagance of his expression, with its self-damaging rationalizing and subjectivism, there is his painful habit of elaborating explicit comparisons. They have to be endured not only by his necessarily tight-lipped enemies, but also by us, and our sympathy turns into resentment.

But the psychological aspect of Richard's character is only one part of his role in the play. When it is stressed to the point of making us forget the rest of Shakespeare's full composition, the result is only a sophisticated version (the king as neurotic) of the popular stereotype of the Bad Ruler. The stage-Richard has tended to illustrate this kind of simplification. One important effect which may be lost when the character of Richard is interpreted in a narrowly psychological fashion is his special relation to the Shakespearian tragic hero. There are tragic qualities in the role which are constantly undercut and thwarted, and this is a part of the play's basic irony. This is missed by Coleridge and others because in dwelling on his neuroticism they tend in effect to scold him for not being more manly and royal, as if the play would be more "successful" if it moved toward a psychological resolution of emotional balance and adjustment. But ironic

---

[6] Edward Dowden, *Shakespeare* (1872), Capricorn reprint (1962), p. 194.

drama succeeds in realizing itself (and here also in interpreting history) to the extent that it dramatizes ethical dilemmas through juxtaposing imperfect values. Thus while Richard's theatrically extravagant language does indeed make us feel that he is emotionally unstable, it may also remind us that violence and hyperbole characterize the speech of the tragic hero; and remembering this, we may observe that the excessive and unsupported rhetoric with which Richard asserts the divinity of kingship not only proves his lack of realism, but also serves like the tragic hero's assertion of transcendent values to counter the forces in the play for a lesser kind of order, such as York's efforts at accommodation or Bolingbroke's effective military government. These forces have their own identifying speech—prosaic, literal, close-mouthed, carefully public and politic—which is in constant contrast with Richard's emotional language.

Similarly, Richard's neuroticism is not only a crippling weakness, but it is also a version of the tragic hero's "madness," and it therefore implies a special kind of power and insight. It is associated with an intuitive awareness about the outcome of events and an acuteness in analyzing the motives of others. By contrast it makes normal people, especially Bolingbroke and Northumberland, appear blunted and insensitive. It seems to force them to face up to the truth about themselves and their ultimate designs, and to say with its intense and peculiar honesty that they are superior only because they do not know or reveal their deeper beings. Richard's intuitive sensing of the motives of Bolingbroke is characteristic: "He helplessly divines Bolingbroke's nebulous purpose and perhaps even shapes that purpose by expressing his willingness to surrender his crown before Bolingbroke, so far as we can see, has consciously entertained the idea of taking it." [7] In the distance, with all its great differences, is the tragic "madness" of Hamlet, which helps him to penetrate the depersonalized court of Claudius and to force it to face its poisoned self. A recognition of the partial resemblance of Richard to Hamlet intensifies our sense of Richard's full character and of the confining ironies of the play itself.

All this and more, by general agreement, is most richly realized in the deposition scenes. Here what could easily remain mere spectacle is charged with dramatic significance by having Richard and Bolingbroke attempt to impose on each other and on the situation their contrary views of its personal and historical meaning. It is as if two plays were contending for the stage. Bolingbroke is already king in fact, but no ceremony will redeem a usurpation; consequently he must

[7] James A. S. McPeek, "Richard and His Shadow World," *The American Imago,* 15 (1958), 204.

attempt, in totalitarian fashion, to ratify or justify his act by staging a confession and renunciation from Richard. "Fetch hither Richard, that in common view/ He may surrender; so we shall proceed/ Without suspicion." This kind of play must be well-made: language and emotion have to be carefully controlled, and nothing spontaneous can be allowed to interfere with the prearranged effects. Bolingbroke's part is to be as patient, just, and royal as possible. The unsympathetic task of forcing Richard to read over the list of his crimes (so that the audience, the commoners, will be satisfied) is naturally delegated to Northumberland. Richard's crimes are real, and Bolingbroke is indeed a more efficient ruler, but there is an inevitable element of mummery in the forced confession, and this affects our judgment and prepares us to feel with Richard what it means to be manipulated and dehumanized. ("What must the king do now?") In this way another side of Richard's theatricality comes into view: he play-acts not to disguise or excuse himself but "to suffer everything that this role demands of him." [8] He deposes himself, as it were, "in some long, agonizing ceremony." [9] The play that he imposes on Bolingbroke's insists that everyone on the stage and in the theater feel with him what it means to be degraded and destroyed. It is natural and appropriate that his "play" should seem improvised rather than well-made, moving on a deep level from image to image, calling as the need develops for stage props like the mirror—a symbol of truth-telling as well as of vanity.[10]

As Richard and Bolingbroke contend for the "stage" it is still clear, however, that they are only parts of Shakespeare's full drama, which is neither the play of the restoration of legal rights and order (as Bolingbroke would have it), nor the play of the betrayal and sacrifice of the anointed king (as Richard insists). The problem-breeding balance of ironic drama and of history viewed as irony is still maintained. The weak side of Richard's theatricality is still present: the emotions of the "suffering king entering the world of the dispossessed" are discussed as well as felt, and a part of his role is that of the stage actor caught removing his make-up ("Alack, why am I sent for . . .") or studying his lines ("I hardly yet have learned . . .").[11] More important and more deeply ironic is the continued association of Richard with something radically opposed to order. He is emotionally sloppy, incapable of keeping his form, the most un-English (or un-Roman)

---

[8] W. H. Clemen, *The Development of Shakespeare's Imagery* (1951), Dramabook reprint, p. 55.

[9] Walter Pater, *Appreciations* (London, 1889), p. 198.

[10] Peter Ure, Intro. to *King Richard II*, New Arden edition (Harvard, 1956), p. lxxxii.

[11] Travis Bogard, "Shakespeare's Second Richard," *PMLA*, LXX (1955), 205–6.

of English kings, and this is given a painful emphasis by his occasional
realization that he is laughed at for his excesses. He has been a callous
perverter and destroyer of the legal forms, the parchment bonds and
the charters of time, which give one kind of order and security to
society. Finally, his relationship to time, or the meaning his career
gives to time, is that of a movement toward formlessness, dissolution,
nothingness. This movement is expressed through plot and character
most obviously, but also through metaphors which reverse their implications so that the fertile earth becomes the dirt of the grave, the
blood of national unity and royal succession becomes the gore of
civil strife, and so on.[12] This movement is more than a "death-wish."
more even than the recognition that the only Lancastrian retirement
plan for a deposed king is murder; it is finally a disbelief in the expressive validity of all "tradition, form, and ceremonious duty." By
contrast, Bolingbroke's mummery at the deposition has this much
virtue: it permits him to act as well as to play-act, and is at least
lip service to the necessity in society of some recognized formal manner of behavior.

Bolingbroke's relation to time, and his character and role generally,
are not easy to define. It has been suggested that the obscurity of his
motives and the relative flatness of his character are a sign that he is
instinctively opportunistic, but this suggestion soon becomes circular
since opportunism is by definition a "tacit vice" [13] and its motives
cannot therefore be openly dramatized. A related suggestion is that
the real Bolingbroke is hidden in the public role—an allegedly inevitable effect of high office on private worth,[14] but this is always in
danger of growing into a satiric leveling interpretation ("We know
who you really are up there.") which is not clearly supported by the
play. It has been suggested, further, that we tend to feel the presence
of "character" only where personality exceeds dramatic role[15] and that
Bolingbroke seems characterless in comparison with Richard because
he is perfectly functional, is only what he has to do in the play and
nothing more. Perhaps these and other suggestions are ways of saying
that despite Bolingbroke's personal and political success in the play
he is as much an inhabitant of its confining ironies as is Richard.
Neither is free.

By his self-deposition Richard does appear, momentarily, to be
free. He is free to turn on the crudely insistent Northumberland:

---

[12] See Richard Altick, "Symphonic Imagery in *Richard II*," *PMLA*, LXII (1947),
339–65.
[13] Brents Stirling, "Bolingbroke's 'Decision,'" *Shakespeare Quarterly*, II (1951),
30.
[14] Palmer, *passim*.
[15] Robert Langbaum, *The Poetry of Experience* (London, 1957), p. 169.

"No lord of thine, thou haught, insulting man,/ Nor no man's lord."
He is free because he has no name or title still to lose; yet the irony
persists: within this freedom he can move not toward growth and
self-realization, but only toward the nothingness of death. When he
looks into the mirror, he foresees that the final "substance" is the
"silence in the tortur'd soul"; and the conclusion of his prison soliloquy is that "Nor I nor any man that but man is/ With nothing shall
be pleas'd, till he be eas'd/ With being nothing." "Richard's actual
death is courageous, or perhaps perfunctory, but it does not alter
this." [16] Nor does Richard's death really free Bolingbroke. His "success" is confined and discolored: "Lords, I protest, my soul is full of
woe/ That blood should sprinkle me to make me grow." To ask if
he is sincere in his protestation is not quite relevant. He is not a
suavely insincere villain like Claudius; he is caught, rather, in the
ironic circumstances which underlie the mode of the play, and therefore at this moment his voice of necessity is public and obscure.

Only one person is free from the enveloping ironies: Prince Hal.
He is reported to be living in the taverns, and when told of the
"triumphs" to be held at Oxford, "His answer was, he would unto
the stews/ And from the common'st creature pluck a glove/ And wear
it as a favor; and with that/ He would unhorse the lustiest chal-
lenger." This is a new tone, strong and cocky, a voice derived from
another legend invented by the people, whose perennial instinct is
to find its young heroes in lucky, off-beat places outside of the gray-
ness of ironic history. We may infer that the nature of such a hero
and how he enters history and changes its mode are to be the subjects of the plays to follow, and that the hero's success will "show
more goodly" by being placed against the "sullen ground" of *Richard II*.

[16] Ure, p. lxxxiii.

Symphonic Imagery in *Richard II*

by Richard D. Altick

Critics on occasion have remarked the peculiar unity of tone which distinguishes *Richard II* from most of Shakespeare's other plays. Walter Pater wrote that, like a musical composition, it possesses "a certain concentration of all its parts, a simple continuity, an evenness in execution, which are rare in the great dramatist. . . . It belongs to a small group of plays, where, by happy birth and consistent evolution, dramatic form approaches to something like the unity of a lyrical ballad, a lyric, a song, a single strain of music." [1] And J. Dover Wilson, in his edition of the play, has observed that "*Richard II* possesses a unity of tone and feeling greater than that attained in many of his greater plays, a unity found, I think, to the same degree elsewhere only in *Twelfth Night, Antony and Cleopatra,* and *The Tempest.*" [2]

How can we account for that impression of harmony, of oneness, which we receive when we read the play or listen to its lines spoken upon the stage? The secret, it seems to me, lies in an aspect of Shakespeare's genius which has oftener been condemned than praised. Critics and casual readers alike have groaned over the fine-drawn ingenuity of the Shakespearean quibble, which, as Dr. Johnson maintained, was "the fatal Cleopatra for which he lost the world, and was content to lose it." But it is essentially the same habit of the creative imagination—a highly sensitized associational gift—that produces iterative symbolism and imagery. Simple word-play results from the poet's awareness of the diverse meanings of words, of which, however, he makes no better use than to demonstrate his own cleverness and to tickle for a moment the wit of the audience. These exhibitions of verbal agility are simply decorations scattered upon the surface of the poetic fabric; they can be ripped out without loss. But suppose

---

"*Symphonic Imagery in* Richard II" *by Richard D. Altick. From* PMLA, 62 (*1947*), *339–352; 361–365. Copyright © 1947 by Publications of the Modern Language Association of America. Reprinted by permission of the Modern Language Association of America.*

[1] "Shakespeare's English Kings," *Appreciations,* library ed. (London, 1910), pp. 202–203.

[2] *Richard II,* ed. J. Dover Wilson (Cambridge, 1939), pp. xiv–xv.

that to the poet's associational sensitivity is added a further awareness
of the multitudinous emotional overtones of words. When he puts
this faculty to use he is no longer merely playing a game; instead,
words have become the shells in which ideas and symbols are en-
closed. Suppose furthermore that instead of being the occupation of
a few fleeting lines of the text, certain words of multifold meanings
are played upon throughout the five acts, recurring time after time
like leitmotivs in music. And suppose finally that this process of
repetition is applied especially to words of sensuous significance, words
that evoke vivid responses in the imagination. When these things
happen to certain words—when they cease to be mere vehicles for a
brief indulgence of verbal fancy and, taking on a burden of serious
meaning, become thematic material—the poet has crossed the border-
line that separates word-play from iterative imagery. Language has
become the willing servant of structure, and what was on other occasions only a source of exuberant but undisciplined wit now is con-
verted to the higher purpose of poetic unity.

That, briefly, is what happens in *Richard II*. The familiar word-
plays of the earlier Shakespearean dramas persist: John of Gaunt puns
endlessly upon his own name. But in this drama a word is not commonly taken up, rapidly revolved, so that all its various facets of
meaning flash out, and then discarded. Instead, certain words are
played upon throughout the drama. Far from being decorations, "gay,
fresh, variegated flowers of speech," as Pater called them,[3] they are
woven deeply into the thought-web of the play. Each word-theme
symbolizes one or another of the fundamental ideas of the story, and
every time it reappears it perceptibly deepens and enriches those
meanings and at the same time charges the atmosphere with emotional
significance.

The most remarkable thing about these leitmotivs is the way in
which they are constantly mingling and coalescing, two or three of
them joining to form a single new figure, very much in the manner
in which "hooked images," as Professor Lowes called them, were
formed in the subconscious mind of Coleridge. This repeated criss-
crossing of familiar images[4] makes of the whole text one vast arabesque of language, just as a dozen lines of *Love's Labour's Lost* form
a miniature arabesque when the poet's quibbling mood is upon him.
And since each image motif represents one of the dominant ideas of
the play (heredity, patriotism, sycophancy, etc.) the coalescing of these
images again and again emphasizes the complex relationship between

[3] *Appreciations*, p. 194.
[4] Throughout this paper I use the words *image* and *imagery* in their most inclu-
sive sense of metaphorical as well as "picture-making" but non-figurative language.

the ideas themselves, so that the reader is kept ever aware that all that happens in *Richard II* results inevitably from the interaction of many elements.

It is pointless to try to explain by further generalizations this subtle and exceedingly intricate weaving together of metaphor and symbol—this glorified word-play, if you will—which is the key to the total poetic effect of *Richard II*. All I can do is to draw from the fabric, one by one, the strands that compose it, and to suggest in some manner the magical way in which they interact and by association and actual fusion reciprocally deepen their meaning.

Miss Spurgeon has pointed out how in *Antony and Cleopatra* the cosmic grandeur of the theme is constantly emphasized by the repetition of the word *world*.[5] In a similar manner the symbolism of *Richard II* is dominated by the related words *earth, land,* and *ground.* In no other play of Shakespeare is the complex of ideas represented by these words so tirelessly dwelt upon.[6] The words are but three in number, and superficially they seem roughly synonymous; but they have many intellectual ramifications, which become more and more meaningful as the play progresses and the words are used first for one thing and then for another. As our experience of the words increases, their connotation steadily deepens. In addition to their obvious meaning in a particular context they come to stand for something larger and more undefinable—a mingling of everything they have represented earlier.

Above all, *earth* is the symbol of the English nation. It is used by Shakespeare to connote those same values which we find in the equivalent synecdoche of *soil,* as in "native soil." It sums up all the feeling inherent in the sense of pride in nation—of jealousy when the country is threatened by foreign incursion, of bitter anger when its health has been destroyed by mismanagement or greed. "This earth of majesty," John of Gaunt calls England in his famous speech, ". . . This blessed plot, this earth, this realm, this England." (II. i. 41, 50)[7] And a few lines farther on: "This land of such dear souls, this dear dear land. . . ." (II. i. 57). Having once appeared, so early in the play, in such lustrous context, the words *earth* and *land* forever after have richer significance. Whenever they recur, they are more meaningful, more powerful. Thus Richard's elaborate speech upon his arrival in Wales—

> As a long-parted mother with her child
> Plays fondly with her tears and smiles in meeting,

---

[5] Caroline F. E. Spurgeon, *Shakespeare's Imagery* (Cambridge, 1936), pp. 352–353.
[6] In *Richard II* the three words occur a total of 71 times.
[7] I am using the text of William A. Neilson and Charles J. Hill (Boston, 1942).

> So, weeping, smiling, greet I thee, my earth,
> And do thee favours with my royal hands.

*   *   *

> Mock not my senseless conjuration, lords.
> This earth shall have a feeling, and these stones
> Prove armed soldiers, ere her native king
> Shall falter under foul rebellion's arms
>
> (III. ii. 8–11, 23–26)

—undoubtedly gains in emotional splendor (as well as dramatic irony) by its reminiscences of John of Gaunt's earlier language. The two men between them make the English earth the chief verbal theme of the play.

Richard, we have just seen, speaks pridefully of *"my* earth." To him, ownership of the land is the most tangible and positive symbol of his rightful kingship. He bids Northumberland tell Bolingbroke that "every stride he makes upon my land/ Is dangerous treason" (III. iii. 92–93), and as he lies dying from the stroke of Exton's sword his last thought is for his land: "Exton, thy fierce hand/ Hath with the king's blood stained the king's own land" (V. v. 110–11). It is only natural, then, that *land* should be the key word in the discussions of England's sorry condition. Symbol of Englishmen's nationalistic pride and of the wealth of kings, it becomes symbol also of Englishmen's shame and kings' disgrace:

> Why, cousin, wert thou regent of the world,
> It were a shame to let this land by lease;
> But for thy world enjoying but this land,
> Is it not more than shame to shame it so?
> Landlord of England art thou now, not king.
>
> (II. 1. 109–113)

Northumberland's sad allusion to "this declining land" (II. i. 240), York's to "this woeful land" (II. ii. 99) and Richard's to "this revolting land" (III. iii. 163) carry on this motif.

But *earth,* while it emblematizes the foundation of kingly pride and power, is also a familiar symbol of the vanity of human life and of what, in the middle ages, was a fascinating illustration of that vanity —the fall of kings. "Men," Mowbray sighs, "are but gilded loam or painted clay" (I. i. 179); and Richard, luxuriating in self-pity, often remembers it; to earth he will return.

> Ah, Richard [says Salisbury], with the eyes of heavy mind
> I see thy glory like a shooting star
> Fall to the base earth from the firmament.
>
> (II. iv. 18–20)

The earth, Richard knows, is accustomed to receive the knees of cour-
tiers: "Fair cousin," he tells Bolingbroke after he has given away his
kingdom for the sheer joy of listening to himself do so, "you debase
your princely knee/ To make the base earth proud with kissing it"
(III. iii. 190–1). And the idea of the ground as the resting place for
suppliant knees, and therefore the antithesis of kingly elevation, is
repeated thrice in the two scenes dealing with Aumerle's conspiracy.[8]

The irony of this association of *earth* with both kingly glory and
abasement is deepened by another role the word has in this earth-
preoccupied play. For after death, earth receives its own; and in
Richard II the common notion of the grave has new meaning, because
the ubiquitous symbol of *earth* embraces it too. By the beginning of
the third act, *earth* has lost its earlier joyful connotation to Richard,
and this king, whose feverish imagination no amount of woe can cool,
eagerly picks up a hint from Scroop:

> *Scroop.*   Those whom you curse
>   Have felt the worst of death's destroying wound
>   And lie full low, grav'd in the hollow ground.
>
>   *   *   *
>
> *Richard.* Let's talk of graves, of worms, and epitaphs;
>   Make dust our paper and with rainy eyes
>   Write sorrow on the bosom of the earth.
>   Let's choose executors and talk of wills;
>   And yet not so; for what can we bequeath
>   Save our deposed bodies to the ground?
>   Our lands, our lives, and all are Bolingbroke's,
>   And nothing can we call our own but death,
>   And that small model of the barren earth
>   Which serves as paste and cover to our bones.
>   For God's sake, let us sit upon the ground
>   And tell sad stories of the death of kings.
>   (III. ii. 138–140, 145–156)

And later, in another ecstasy of self-pity, he conjures up an elaborate
image of making some pretty match with shedding tears:

> As thus, to drop them still upon one place,
> Till they have fretted us a pair of graves
> Within the earth.   (III. iii. 166–168)

---

[8] The much admired little passage about the roan Barbary takes on added poignancy when the other overtones of *ground* are remembered:
> *King Richard.* Rode he on Barbary? Tell me, gentle friend,
>   How went he under him?
> *Groom.* So proudly as if he disdain'd the ground.
>   (V.v. 81–83)

The same association occurs in the speeches of the other characters. Surrey, casting his gage at Fitzwater's feet, envisions his father's skull lying quietly in earth (IV. i. 66–69); a moment or two later the Bishop of Carlisle brings news that the banished Mowbray, having fought for Jesu Christ in glorious Christian field, "at Venice gave/ His body to that pleasant country's earth" (IV. i. 97–8); and in the same scene Richard, having handed over his crown to the usurper, exclaims,

> Long mayst thou live in Richard's seat to sit,
> And soon lie Richard in an earthy pit!
>   (IV. i. 218–219)

A final theme in the symphonic pattern dominated by the symbol of earth is that of the untended garden. Miss Spurgeon has adequately emphasized the importance of this iterated image in the history plays, and, as she points out, it reaches its climax in *Richard II,* particularly in the allegorical scene of the Queen's garden.[9] In Shakespeare's imagination the misdeeds of Richard and his followers constituted an overwhelming indignity to the precious English earth—to a nation which, in happier days, had been a sea-wall'd garden. And thus the play is filled with references to ripeness and the seasons, to planting and cropping and plucking and reaping, to furrows and plowing, and caterpillars and withered bay trees and thorns and flowers.[10]

Among the host of garden images in the play, one especially is unforgettable because of the insistence with which Shakespeare thrice echoes it. It is the terrible metaphor of the English garden being drenched by showers of blood.

> I'll use the advantage of my power
> And lay the summer's dust with showers of blood
> Rain'd from the wounds of slaughtered Englishmen;
>   (III. iii. 42–44)

threatens Bolingbroke as he approaches Flint castle; and when the King himself appears upon the walls, he casts the figure back in Bolingbroke's face:

> But ere the crown he looks for live in peace,
> Ten thousand bloody crowns of mothers' sons
> Shall ill become the flower of England's face,
> Change the complexion of her maid-pale peace

---

[9] *Shakespeare's Imagery,* pp. 216–224.
[10] We must not, of course, take *garden* too literally. Shakespeare obviously intended the term in its wider metaphorical sense of fields and orchards.

To scarlet indignation, and bedew
Her pastures' grass with faithful English blood.
                                   (III. iii. 95–100)

The Bishop of Carlisle takes up the theme:

And if you crown him, let me prophesy,
The blood of English shall manure the ground,
And future ages groan for this foul act.
                                   (IV. i. 136–138)

And the new King—amply justifying Professor Van Doren's remark
that not only are most of the characters in this play poets, but they
copy one another on occasion[11]—echoes it:

Lords, I protest, my soul is full of woe
That blood should sprinkle me to make me grow.
                                   (V. vi. 45–46)

This extraordinary series of four images is one of the many examples of the manner in which the principal symbols of *Richard II* so
often chime together, bringing the ideas they represent into mo-
mentary conjunction and thus compounding those single emotional
strains into new and revealing harmonies. In this case the "showers
of blood" metaphor provides a recurrent nexus between the pervasive
symbol of earth and another, equally pervasive, symbol: that of blood.

Both Professor Bradley[12] and Miss Spurgeon[13] have pointed out the
splendid horror which Shakespeare achieves in *Macbeth* by his repeated allusions to blood. Curiously enough, the word *blood,* together
with such related words as *bloody* and *bleed,* occurs much less fre-
quently in *Macbeth* than it does in most of the history plays. What
gives the word the tremendous force it undoubtedly possesses in *Macbeth* is not the frequency with which it is spoken, but rather the
intrinsic magnificence of the passages in which it appears and the
fact that in this play it has but one significance—the literal one. In
the history plays, however, the word *blood* plays two major roles.
Often it has the same meaning it has in *Macbeth,* for these too are
plays in which men's minds often turn toward the sword:

. . . our kingdom's earth should not be soil'd
With that dear blood which it hath fostered
                                   (I. iii. 125–126)

says Richard in one more instinctive (and punning!) association of

[11] Mark Van Doren, *Shakespeare* (New York, 1939), p. 88.
[12] A. C. Bradley, *Shakespearean Tragedy,* 2d edition (London, 1905), pp. 335–356.
[13] *Shakespeare's Imagery,* p. 334.

blood and earth. But *blood* in the history plays also stands figuratively for inheritance, descent, familial pride; and this is the chief
motivating theme of the play—the right of a monarch of unquestionably legitimate blood to his throne. The two significances constantly
interplay, giving the single word a new multiple connotation wherever
it appears. The finest instance of this merging of ideas is in the
Duchess of Gloucester's outburst to John of Gaunt. Here we have an
elaborate contrapuntal metaphor, the basis of which is a figure derived from the familiar medieval genealogical symbol of the Tree of
Jesse, and which is completed by a second figure of the seven vials of
blood. The imposition of the figure involving the word *blood* (in its
literal and therefore most vivid use) upon another figure which for
centuries embodied the concept of family descent, thus welds together with extraordinary tightness the word and its symbolic significance. The occurrence of *blood* in other senses on the borders of
the metaphor (in the first and next-to-last lines of the passage) helps
to focus attention upon the process occurring in the metaphor itself.

> Hath love in thy old blood no living fire?
> Edward's seven sons, whereof thyself art one,
> Were as seven vials of his sacred blood,
> Or seven fair branches springing from one root.
> Some of those seven are dried by nature's course,
> Some of those branches by the Destinies cut;
> But Thomas, my dear lord, my life, my Gloucester,
> One vial full of Edward's sacred blood,
> One flourishing branch of his most royal root,
> Is crack'd, and all the precious liquor spilt,
> Is hack'd down, and his summer leaves all faded,
> By Envy's hand and Murder's bloody axe.
> Ah, Gaunt, his blood was thine!
>
> (I. ii. 10–22)

Because it has this multiple function, the word *blood* in this play
loses much of the concentrated vividness and application it has in
Macbeth, where it means but one unmistakable thing; but its ambiguity here gives it a new sort of power. If it is less effective as
imagery, it does serve to underscore the basic idea of the play, that
violation of the laws of blood descent leads but to the spilling of
precious English blood. That is the meaning of the word as it pulses
from beginning to end, marking the emotional rhythm of the play.

In *Richard II,* furthermore, the word has an additional, unique
use, one which involves an especially striking symbol. It has often
been remarked how Shakespeare, seizing upon a hint in his sources,
plays upon Richard's abnormal tendency to blanch and blush. In the

imagery thus called forth, *blood* has a prominent part. How, demands the haughty king of John of Gaunt, dare thou

> with thy frozen admonition
> Make pale our cheek, chasing the royal blood
> With fury from his native residence.
>
> (II. i. 117–119)

And when the King hears the news of the Welshmen's defection, Aumerle steadies his quaking body:

> Comfort, my liege; why looks your Grace so pale?
> *Richard.* But now the blood of twenty thousand men
> Did triumph in my face, and they are fled;
> And, till so much blood thither come again,
> Have I not reason to look pale and dead?
>
> (III. ii. 75–79)

This idiosyncrasy of the King is made the more vivid because the imagery of the play constantly refers to pallor, even in contexts far removed from him. The Welsh captain reports that "the pale-fac'd moon looks bloody on the earth" (II. iv. 10). In another speech, the words *pale* and *blood,* though not associated in a single image, occur so close to each other that it is tempting to suspect an habitual association in Shakespeare's mind:

> Pale trembling coward, there I throw my gage,
> Disclaiming here the kindred of the King,
> And lay aside my high blood's royalty.
>
> (I. i. 69–71)

And as we have already seen, the King prophesied that "ten thousand bloody crowns of mothers' sons/ Shall . . . change the complexion of [England's] maid-pale peace" (III. iii. 96–98). Elsewhere Bolingbroke speaks of "pale beggar-fear" (I. i. 189); the Duchess of Gloucester accuses John of Gaunt of "pale cold cowardice" (I. ii. 34); and York describes how the returned exile and his army fright England's "pale-fac'd villages" with war (II. iii. 94).

The idea of pallor and blushing is linked in turn with what is perhaps the most famous image-motif of the play, that of Richard (or the fact of his kingship) emblematized by the sun. More attention probably has been paid to the sun-king theme than it is worth, for although it occurs in two very familiar passages, it contributes far less to the harmonic unity of the play than do a number of other symbol strains. In any event, the conjunction of the sun image with that of blushing provides one more evidence of the closeness with which the poetic themes of the play are knit together. In the first of

the sun-king speeches, Richard compares himself, at the length to
which he is addicted, with "the searching eye of heaven" (III. ii. 37).
Finally, after some ten lines of analogy:

> So when this thief, this traitor, Bolingbroke,
> Who all this while hath revell'd in the night
> Whilst we were wand'ring with the antipodes,
> Shall see us rising in our throne, the east,
> His treasons will sit blushing in his face. . . .
>   (III. ii. 47–51)

And Bolingbroke in a later scene does him the sincere flattery of imi-
tation:

> See, see, King Richard doth himself appear,
> As doth the blushing discontented sun
> From out the fiery portal of the east.
>   (III. iii. 62–64)

Another occurrence of the sun image provides a link with the pervasive motif of tears. Salisbury, having envisioned Richard's glory
falling to the base earth from the firmament, continues:

> Thy sun sets weeping in the lowly west,
> Witnessing storms to come, woe, and unrest.
>   (II. iv. 21–22)

In no other history play is the idea of tears and weeping so insistently
presented.[14] It is this element which enforces most strongly our impression of Richard as a weakling, a monarch essentially feminine in
nature, who has no conception of stoic endurance or resignation but
a strong predilection for grief. This is why the play seems so strangely
devoid of the heroic; the King and Queen are too much devoted to
luxuriating in their misery, and the other characters find a morbid
delight in at least alluding to unmanly tears.

Professor Van Doren, in his sensitive essay on *Richard II,* elo-
quently stresses the importance of the word *tongue* in the play.[15]
Tongue, he says, is the key word of the piece. I should prefer to give
that distinction to *earth;* but there is no denying the effectiveness of
Shakespeare's tireless repetition of the idea of speech, not only by
the single word *tongue* but also by such allied words as *mouth, speech,*
and *word.* A few minutes' study of Bartlett's *Concordance* will show
that *Richard II* is unique in this insistence upon the concept of

---

[14] There are many more references to tears and weeping in *Titus Andronicus,* but
the obvious inferiority of the poetry and the crudity of characterization make their
presence far less remarkable.

[15] *Shakespeare,* pp. 85–87.

speech; that the word *tongue* occurs here oftener than in any other play is but one indication.

This group of associated words heavily underscores two leading ideas in the play. In the first place, it draws constant attention to the propensity for verbalizing (as Shakespeare would not have called it!) which is Richard's fatal weakness. He cannot bring himself to live in a world of hard actuality; the universe to him is real only as it is presented in packages of fine words. Aumerle tries almost roughly to recall him from his weaving of sweet, melancholy sounds to a realization of the crucial situation confronting him, but he rouses himself only momentarily and then relapses into a complacent enjoyment of the sound of his own tongue. It is of this trait that we are constantly reminded as all the characters regularly use periphrases when they must speak of what they or others have said. By making the physical act of speech, the sheer fact of language, so conspicuous, they call attention to its illusory nature—to the vast difference between what the semanticists call the intensional and extensional universes. That words are mere conventional sounds moulded by the tongue, and reality is something else again, is constantly on the minds of all the characters. The initial dispute between Mowbray and Bolingbroke is "the bitter clamour of two eager tongues" (I. i. 49); Mowbray threatens to cram his antagonist's lie "through the false passage of thy throat" (I. i. 125); and later, in a fine cadenza, he conceives of his eternal banishment in terms of the engaoling of his tongue, whose "use is to me no more/ Than an unstringed viol or a harp," and concludes:

> What is thy sentence [then] but speechless death,
> Which robs my tongue from breathing native breath?
> (I. iii. 161–162, 172–173)

Bolingbroke, for his part, marvels over the power of a single word to change the lives of men:

> How long a time lies in one little word!
> Four lagging winters and four wanton springs
> End in a word: such is the breath of kings.
> (I. iii. 213–215)

Gaunt too is preoccupied with tongues and speech; and when Aumerle returns from his farewell with Bolingbroke, from tears the image theme swiftly turns to tongues:

> *Richard.* What said our cousin when you parted with him?
> *Aumerle.* "Farewell!"

> And, for my heart disdained that my tongue
> Should so profane the word, that taught me craft
> To counterfeit oppression of such grief
> That words seem'd buried in my sorrow's grave.
> Marry, would the word "farewell" have length'ned hours
> And added years to his short banishment,
> He should have had a volume of farewells.
>
> (I. iv. 10–18)

And we have but reached the end of Act I; the remainder of the play is equally preoccupied with the unsubstantiality of human language.[16]

But the unremitting stress laid upon tongues and words in this play serves another important end: it reminds us that Richard's fall is due not only to his preference for his own words rather than for deeds, but also to his blind predilection for comfortable flattery rather than sound advice. Words not only hypnotize, suspend the sense of reality: they can sting and corrupt. And so the tongues of *Richard II* symbolize also the honeyed but poisonous speech of the sycophants who surround him. "No," replies York to Gaunt's suggestion that his dying words might yet undeaf Richard's ear,

> it is stopp'd with other flattering sounds,
> As praises, of whose taste the wise are found,
> Lascivious metres, to whose venom sound
> The open ear of youth doth always listen.
>
> (II. i. 17–20)

The venom to which York refers and the snake which produces it form another theme of the imagery of this play. The snake-venom motif closely links the idea of the garden on the one hand (for what grossly untended garden would be without its snakes?) and the idea of the tongue on the other. All three meet in the latter part of Richard's speech in III. ii:

> But let thy spiders, that suck up thy venom,
> And heavy-gaited toads lie in their way,
> Doing annoyance to the treacherous feet
> Which with usurping steps do trample thee

---

[16] Another way in which Shakespeare adds to the constant tragic sense of unsubstantiality in this play—the confusion of appearance and reality—is the repeated use of the adjective *hollow*, especially in connection with death: "our hollow parting" (I. iv. 9), the "hollow womb" of the grave (II. i. 83), "the hollow eyes of death" (II. i. 270), a grave set in "the hollow ground" (III. ii. 140), "the hollow crown" in which Death keeps his court (III. ii. 160).

Yield stinging nettles to mine enemies;
And when they from thy bosom pluck a flower,
Guard it, I pray thee, with a lurking adder
Whose double tongue may with a mortal touch
Throw death upon thy sovereign's enemies.

(III. ii. 14–22)

And the double association occurs again in the garden scene, when
the Queen demands of the gardener,

Thou, old Adam's likeness, set to dress this garden,
How dares thy harsh rude tongue sound this unpleasing news?
What Eve, what serpent, hath suggested thee
To make a second fall of cursed man?   (III. iv. 73–76)

Mowbray elsewhere speaks of "slander's venom'd spear" (I. i. 171), and
to Richard, the flatterers who have deserted him are, naturally
enough, "villains, vipers, damn'd without redemption!/ . . . Snakes, in
my heart-blood warm'd, that sting my heart!" (III. ii. 129–131). . . .

A final aspect of the use of iterative imagery in *Richard II* is the
manner in which a particularly important passage is prepared for by
the interweaving into the poetry, long in advance, of inconspicuous
but repeated hints of the imagery which is to dominate that passage.
The method is exactly analogous to that by which in a symphony a
melody appears, at first tentatively, indeed almost unnoticed, first in
one choir of the orchestra, then another, until ultimately it comes to
its reward as the theme of a climactic section. In such a manner is the
audience prepared, although unconsciously, for Richard's last grandi-
ose speech. One takes little note of the first timid appearance of a
reference to beggary or bankruptcy in Bolingbroke's "Or with pale
beggar-fear impeach my height" (I. i. 189). But in the second act the
motif recurs:

Be York the next that must be bankrupt so!
Though death be poor, it ends a mortal woe,
(II. i. 151–152)

and a hundred lines later the idea is repeated: "The king's grown
bankrupt, like a broken man" (II. i. 257). The haunting dread of
destitution, then, however obliquely alluded to, is a recurrent theme,
and adds its small but perceptible share to the whole atmosphere of
impending disaster. It forms the burden of two plaints by Richard
midway in the play:

Let's choose executors and talk of wills;
And yet not so; for what can we bequeath

> Save our deposed bodies to the ground?
> Our lands, our lives and all are Bolingbroke's.
> > (III. ii. 148–151)

> I'll give my jewels for a set of beads,
> My gorgeous palace for a hermitage,
> My gay apparel for an almsman's gown,
> My figur'd goblets for a dish of wood,
> My sceptre for a palmer's walking-staff,
> My subjects for a pair of carved saints,
> And my large kingdom for a little grave.
> > (III. iii. 147–153)

But the time is not ripe for the climactic utterance of this motif. It disappears, to return for a moment in a verbal hint in the deposition scene:

> Let it command a mirror hither straight,
> That it may show me what a face I have
> Since it is bankrupt of his majesty.
> > (IV. i. 265–267)

> Being so great, I have no need to beg.
> > (IV. i. 309)

The Duchess of York momentarily takes up the motif: "A beggar begs that never begg'd before" (V. iii. 78), and Bolingbroke replies:

> Our scene is alt'red from a serious thing,
> And now chang'd to "The Beggar and the King."
> > (V. iii. 79–80)

And now finally come the climax toward which these fleeting references have been pointing: a climax which illuminates the purpose and direction of the earlier talk about beggary and bankruptcy:

> Thoughts tending to content flatter themselves
> That they are not the first of fortune's slaves,
> Nor shall not be the last; like silly beggars
> Who, sitting in the stocks, refuge their shame,
> That many have and others must sit there;
> And in this thought they find a kind of ease,
> Bearing their own misfortunes on the back
> Of such as have before endur'd the like.
> Thus play I in one person many people,
> And none contented. Sometimes am I king;
> Then treasons make me wish myself a beggar;

And so I am. Then crushing penury
Persuades me I was better when a king.

(V. v. 23–35)

And thus from beginning to end *Richard II* is, in a double sense
of which Shakespeare would have approved, a play on words. As
countless writers have affirmed, it is entirely fitting that this should be
so. King Richard, a poet *manqué,* loved words more dearly than he
did his kingdom, and his tragedy is made the more moving by the
style, half rhetorical, half lyrical, in which it is told. Splendid words,
colorful metaphors, pregnant poetic symbols in this drama possess
their own peculiar irony.

But the language of *Richard II,* regarded from the viewpoint I have
adopted in this paper, has another significance, entirely apart from
its appropriateness to theme. It suggests the existence of a vital relationship between two leading characteristics of Shakespeare's poetic
style: the uncontrolled indulgence of verbal wit in the earlier plays
and the use of great image-themes in the plays of his maturity. As I
suggested in the beginning, word-play and iterative imagery are but
two different manifestations of a single faculty in the creative imagination—an exceedingly well developed sense of association. In *Richard II* we see the crucial intermediate stage in the development, or
perhaps more accurately the utilization, of Shakespeare's singular as-
sociative gift. In such passages as John of Gaunt's speech upon his
name, we are reminded of the plays which preceded this from Shakespeare's pen. But, except on certain occasions when they contribute
to the characterization of the poet-king, the brief coruscations of
verbal wit which marked the earlier plays are less evident than
formerly. On the other hand, when we stand back and view the play
as a whole, its separate movements bound so closely together by image
themes, we are enabled to anticipate the future development of Shakespeare's art. The technique that is emerging in *Richard II* is the technique that eventually will have its part in producing the poetry of
Lear and *Macbeth* and *Othello.* Here we have the method: the tricks
of repetition, of cumulative emotional effect, of interweaving and
reciprocal coloration. What is yet to come is the full mastery of the
artistic possibilities of such a technique. True, thanks to its tightly
interwoven imagery *Richard II* has a poetic unity that is unsurpassed
in any of the great tragedies; so far as structure is concerned, Shakespeare has levied from iterative language about all the aid that it will
give. The great improvement will come in another region. Taken in-
dividually, in *Richard II* Shakespeare's images lack the qualities which
they will possess in the later plays. They are, many of them, too conventional for our tastes; they are marred by diffuseness; they bear too

many lingering traces of Shakespeare's affection for words for words' sake. The ultimate condensation, the compression of a universe of meaning into a single bold metaphor, remains to be achieved. But in the best imagery of *Richard II*, especially in those passages which combine several themes into a richly complex pattern of meaning, we receive abundant assurance that Shakespeare will be equal to his task. The process of welding language and thought into a single entity is well begun.

Introduction to *Richard II*

by Peter Ure

. . . The contrast between Bolingbroke as an efficient ruler and Richard as an unwise one contributes to the play's structure and helps to balance the last phase against the first. But a similar balance is not found in that region where deeper motives and sanctions greater than that of physical power are exposed; it is Richard who brings these to life and awareness; against his exposition of them we cannot set the outward man who is Bolingbroke—his impulses are hidden from us; his conduct is ambiguous, partly because such ambiguity is for him an instrument of policy and partly, perhaps, because of his creator's irresolution. "To find out right with wrong—it may not be," says York: Bolingbroke's apparent total unawareness of the dilemma may be due to a settled determination to get what he wants at the cost of ignoring it or merely to Shakespeare's unwillingness to sound his motives too deeply. Whatever the reason, the effect—and this perhaps is the calculation that lies behind the whole unbalance—is to throw all the light upon Richard: his "right" is the burden of his thoughts, and he is the uninterrupted expositor of it.

He introduces the theme in the central scenes of the third Act. His inability to resist Bolingbroke or his demands sets him free, as it were, both to fall back upon the divinity of his kingship as a last resource and to bring it to our awareness, not as a mere theory of sovereignty, but as an active component in the situation as a whole and in his own suffering. In its former relation, York had begun to propound the theme in the preceding Act: Bolingbroke and his company are rebels, *nemine contradicente*; neither their power, nor York's inability to resist it, cancels out the fact of their treason:

> I cannot mend it, I must needs confess,
> Because my power is weak and all ill left.
> But if I could, by Him that gave me life,

> I would attach you all, and make you stoop
> Unto the sovereign mercy of the king;

York speaks as a subject, as Carlisle is later to do. When this theme of powerless, but divinely ordained, right overcome by powerful wrong is transferred from the subject, who infers from it the future punishment of the sinners, to the king himself, who incarnates the right, and is transmuted by his personality, it becomes at once a spring of faith and a cause of suffering. By its nature, since it supposes that the rightful king is a deputy appointed by God and not by the election of power, it is a faith which supports Richard when power is diminished or gone:

> show us the hand of God
> That hath dismiss'd us from our stewardship;
> For well we know no hand of blood and bone
> Can gripe the sacred handle of our sceptre,
> Unless he do profane, steal, or usurp.
> And though you think that all, as you have done,
> Have torn their souls by turning them from us,
> And we are barren and bereft of friends,
> Yet know, my master, God omnipotent,
> Is mustering in his clouds, on our behalf,
> Armies of pestilence, and they shall strike
> Your children yet unborn, and unbegot,
> That lift your vassal hands against my head,
> And threat the glory of my precious crown.

But it is a faith which is, as faiths generally are, at times held with this kind of sublime and richly figured confidence, but at other times has to struggle in Richard's mind with the facts that seem to contradict it: in this case, the paradox of the rightful king who is without power to substantiate his right. Thus arises Richard's suffering. There is a kind of denial of his faith which springs from the difficulty of holding it when the startling fact of the *king's* helplessness seems to mock at its truth or efficacy:

> Cover your heads, and mock not flesh and blood
> With solemn reverence; throw away respect,
> Tradition, form, and ceremonious duty;
> For you have but mistook me all this while.
> I live with bread like you, feel want,
> Taste grief, need friends—subjected thus,
> How can you say to me, I am a king?

Richard suffers, too, in performing the acts which his dilemma enforces upon him because they make him conscious of their contradiction of his claims:

> O God! O God! that e'er this tongue of mine,
> That laid the sentence of dread banishment
> On yon proud man, should take it off again
> With words of sooth

and this leads to the striving to escape from the dilemma, the wish to be no longer the "god on earth" who is so manifestly at the mercy of his subjects:

> O that I were as great
> As is my grief, or lesser than my name!
> Or that I could forget what I have been!
> Or not remember what I must be now!

Yet Richard can recover from this mood enough to affirm the confidences of the next scene, to collapse again, and in the end, even after his resignation, to feel that his own act has betrayed his faith and to suffer because he seems to have committed a kind of voluntary apostasy:

> Mine eyes are full of tears, I cannot see.
> And yet salt water blinds them not so much
> But they can see a sort of traitors here.
> Nay, if I turn mine eyes upon myself,
> I find myself a traitor with the rest.
> For I have given here my soul's consent
> T'undeck the pompous body of a king;
> Made glory base, and sovereignty a slave;
> Proud majesty a subject, state a peasant.

These alternating states, this personal accent and hypertension of grief surely result from Shakespeare's attempt to give us a man who is really suffering. The kind of attention, or the degree of respect, we pay to this suffering will partly depend on our estimate of how far Shakespeare established Bolingbroke's ascendancy in physical power and Richard's weakness as a ruler early in the play. I have suggested that the design is in fact of this kind, leaving the last half of the play largely occupied with the fate of a king deprived of power through his own defects (which are measured against their absence in Bolingbroke) yet hedged about with divinity. If this issue seemed important enough to Shakespeare for it to shape his design and be built into the fabric of his protagonist, Richard's agonies over it are evidently amongst the things which the dramatist wanted us to contemplate at length and in detail. The very fact that we have been encouraged early and firmly to decide that Richard is deficient in the qualities that nourish kingship suggests that we are now to see him as a king who is tragic because this deficiency, and its consequence in loss of power, has not freed him, for himself at least, from the burden of majesty.

It is to make us pay attention to this that Shakespeare at first takes sides between Bolingbroke and Richard, making the latter quickly and deservedly lose power and even underlining the success of the former as ruler. He does this not for the sake of making a political point but in order to create the conditions of outer and inner turbulence proper to a protagonist of stature. Through them the protagonist's sufferings become not merely those of a prince who falls pathetically from high place into darkness, like the heroes of the old *casus* stories, but also those of one in whom belief strives with weakness within while enemies without affront it by their power to force him, as they eventually do, to seem to deny it by his own acts. Similarly, the purpose of Richard's speeches on the inviolability of his right, delivered against the background of Bolingbroke's advancing army and of total loss of power, is not to proclaim the Tudor doctrine of majesty in the teeth of the odds, nor even, as Irving Ribner suggests,[1] to make it sound silly, but to tell us what Richard is feeling and move us with the spectacle. This also is the purpose of Richard's collapses into despair and repudiations under stress. The alternating moods go to make up a man rather than to expose the relativity of a doctrine. It is the design that makes all this life in the character possible by bringing about at an early stage the condition: unarmed and deficient majesty versus armed and able usurpation. It is doubtful if we can even ask about this play Ribner's question "What is the precise political position taken by Shakespeare in the conflict between Richard II and Bolingbroke?,"[2] because this is a question about the condition artificially detached from the character which is its reason for being.

But just as Richard's miscalculations and capricious fancy give us an insight into his weakness, so the kind of attention we pay to his sufferings will be to some extent determined by what commentators have diagnosed as the theatricality with which he expresses them. "He throws himself into the part of the deposed monarch," says Pater, "[and] falls gracefully as on the world's stage."[3] Here again we are in danger of confusing Shakespeare's medium, which is a play designed to cast light above all others on to Richard, with the dramatic character. The gracefulness, the enthusiasm, the loquacity, the taking of the centre of the stage and the consciousness of onlookers are Shakespeare's own

---

[1] "The Political Problem in Shakespeare's Lancastrian Tetralogy," *S.P.*, XLIX (1952), 179–81.

[2] *Ibid.*, p. 171.

[3] "Shakespeare's English Kings" in *Appreciations* (1944 edn), p. 206; Chambers thinks that Richard is "himself a born actor," and Craig (op. cit., p. 128) that he "spent his life not living, but playing parts."

powers and the means which he uses to give us Richard as fully and centrally as he can; they are not attributes of the character, for Richard is no
more an actor than he is a poet.[4] We are not to suppose that because a
character in a play speaks a great deal, he is necessarily fond of the
sound of his own voice, or because he continually takes the centre of the
stage, that he necessarily enjoys playing a part. The Richard who luxu-
riates in his own destruction is a product of some such suppositions; it
also springs from an unwillingness to recognize the appeal of the tradition of the "complaint" and *The Mirror for Magistrates*, from which
Richard's lamentations and reproaches in part descend.[5] It is not
Richard who stages the impressive and symbolical scenes in which he
appears, as G. A. Bonnard claims,[6] but Shakespeare, who desired to set
before us the honoured spectacle of the fallen king.

There is another way in which play-acting or theatricality may be
said to be an element in the character. The scenes, including the deposition scene, in which Richard appears in the last half of the play are
stage-managed by Bolingbroke in the sense that his power and decisions
prescribe the scope of Richard's actions. Richard must play the part
set down for him, and he shows from time to time a weary and baffled
consciousness of this: "What must the king do now?" (III. iii. 143 ff).
The bitter irony is manifest if we remember Queen Elizabeth's remark
on her death-bed about "must" not being a word which may be used
to princes.

> What says King Bolingbroke? Will his Majesty
> Give Richard leave to live till Richard die?
> You make a leg, and Bolingbroke says "ay."

Here Richard caricatures the set nature of the charaters' behaviour.
That actions previously planned are now being performed is emphasized, especially in the deposition scene, by the way in which they are
represented as done for the benefit of an audience within the play:

> Fetch hither Richard, that in common view
> He may surrender;

[4] No more—and no less—than Brutus or Cassius. All are conscious of "bearing a
part," their role in life. There is an element of theatricality in Richard just as there
is an element of corrupt fancy: but to describe Richard as an actor is to allow a
useful metaphor to get out of control. The same thing happens when we describe
him as a poet. It is not helpful to say that he is playing the part of a fallen king
when he *is* a fallen king, even though we may consider that his behaviour in that
condition is unmanly or consciously overdone; he does not bleed in sport; cf. Clemen,
op. cit., p. 55; and for a similar point about Macbeth, K. Muir's Arden edn of *Mac.*,
p. lx.

[5] See W. Farnham, *Medieval Heritage of Elizabethan Tragedy* (Berkeley, 1936),
pp. 416 ff.

[6] "The actor in Richard II," *Shakespeare-Fahrbuch*, lxxxvii–lxxxviii (1952), 99.

Richard is to confess his crimes in order that men may "deem" that
he is "worthily deposed" (IV. i. 227) or "the commons will not then be
satisfied" (IV. i. 272). Bolingbroke is the silent *régisseur*, who intervenes
only occasionally to modify the course of the piece. And we learn from
York how marked is this element of staging in Richard's humiliation
(V. ii. 23 ff). The device emphasizes the helpless yet central position
of Richard, the man with the pistol at his ribs.

Bolingbroke, as Leonard F. Dean expresses it,[7] has in this way turned
the state itself into a theatre; he has assigned his part to Northumberland, and, in the deposition scene, he has set down a part for Richard,
too, to play. From Bolingbroke's point of view, if it is true that the
seizure of power is all that matters to him, Richard has become, indeed, a mere actor in his play, since, in resigning his crown before the
assembled parliament and placing it in the usurper's hands, he pas-
sively does what is expected of him. If it is true that Bolingbroke cares
nothing about the divine sanctions of power, the way in which Richard
performs the act—emphasizing his own grief (IV. i. 191 ff) and shame
(IV. i. 245 ff) and betrayal (IV. i. 233 ff)—hardly amounts to more than
a nuisance, an indulgence in sorrow springing from the weakness of
temper that made Richard a bad king; it is sentimentalizing, and confirms Bolingbroke in what we may suppose to be his view that the
Name without the reality is a shadow without substance: let Richard
be king of sorrows if he will, Bolingbroke will be king in England. But
Bolingbroke's "play" is not Shakespeare's, and it is a mistake, made by
some commentators, to suppose that the two coincide. The Bishop's
prophecy preceding the act of discrowning (IV. i. 136 ff), the conspiracy
that follows it, Richard's warning to Northumberland (V. i. 55 ff), and,
of course, Henry IV's own disturbed conscience later on, show something of the woe that has been engendered and make it plain that, if
Bolingbroke takes the Name to be only a shadow, disarmed before the
untitled holder of power and of no force in politics, Shakespeare does
not, and never expected his audiences to do so either.

It is not only this which shows that our point of view is not to be
identified with the attempt to reduce Richard's status to that of mere
play-actor. For, except on the level of his confirmation in real power
through a public act of abdication, the level of his immediate concern,
Bolingbroke is actually in very imperfect control of his leading actor.
It is the contrast between what Richard has to do with the way he does
it that brings out the shocking paradox of the *helpless king,* the king
who "must." Marlowe's play has this too:

> They give me bread and water being a king

7 *"Richard II:* the State and the Image of the Theatre," *P.M.L.A.,* LXVII (1952).

and it has been Richard's area of suffering ever since he was introduced in his more expressive form in III. ii. But here it is climactic; for
in this scene, by performing what Pater called an "inverted rite," [8]
the king must shed the glory of his name and so, as it were, try to
shatter the paradox that has caused him to suffer and yet, because one
part of it affirmed his right, has allowed him to hope. We can imagine,
perhaps, that Bolingbroke would have liked to run the deposition as
he managed the execution of the favourites, or to contrive some effect
akin to that of the challenge scenes of the first Act, where, as I have
suggested, the stiffness of the language and gestures argues that the
characters are following obediently a procedure laid down in advance.
But Richard, so far as the audience is concerned, knocks awry Bolingbroke's carefully staged professional spectacle. With all the weaknesses
of his feminine sensibility and capricious fancy upon him, he moves
us to pity in verse the contrast of which with the formal vigour of the
verse in the challenge scenes is the measure of Shakespeare's attempt
to give him the voice of a man who is really in pain. And this remains
true even though Shakespeare learnt later on, in *Lear,* to write verse
which is much more expressive of the agonies of fallen majesty.

The episode of the looking-glass towards the end of the deposition
scene is the most remarkable of Richard's departures from the role set
down for him by Bolingbroke. It wrenches attention inwards to Richard, the more designedly in that it seems to complete a movement apparent throughout the whole scene. This begins in a very public and
external way with the yells and threats of the appellants, modulates to
Carlisle's appeal to God and men's consciences, and thence to Richard's
profoundly personal rendering of the formal act of abdication, in which
the crown becomes an image of his grief (IV. i. 181–9) and the by-
standers not witnesses but participators in a crime (IV. i. 167–75).
Northumberland tries to drag Richard back towards the public and the
formal, towards Bolingbroke's "theatre"; but the movement, with
Richard in command of it, has gathered too much momentum, and his
efforts are in vain. Richard sends for the looking-glass, the double-
edged symbol of vanity and truth-telling.[9]

[8] "It is as if Shakespeare had had in mind some inverted rite, like those old ecclesi-
astical or military ones, by which human hardness, or human justice, adds the last
touch of unkindness to the execution of its sentences," op. cit., p. 205.

[9] As iconographers have shown, the mirror is the attribute of *Vanitas*: on this, see
G. F. Hartlaub, *Zauber des Spiegels* (Munich, 1951) and H. Schwarz, "The Mirror
in Art," *Art Quarterly* (Detroit), xv (1952), 97–118. The epithet which Richard uses
for it, *flattering* (and therefore lying) is very commonly attached to looking-glasses
of any kind: e.g. in Lyly, Daniel, Heywood, Webster, and Burton (for references see
my article in *P.Q.*, XXXIV (1955), 220); Elizabeth I on her death-bed rejected a "flattering" glass and called for a "true" one (see Nichols, op. cit., III. 614). The mirror also
has the property of reflecting the true state of things: hence its use as a book-title

The episode points forward to the solitary and self-communing Richard of the prison soliloquy. There is something deliberately unexplained, something therefore impulsive and compulsive, about his wish to have the mirror at this moment, and something intense and private in his act of looking at it, for this, too, is a kind of soliloquy, his first. It is also thematically linked with the prison soliloquy in that it touches the question whether Richard, in divesting himself of the name of king, has anything at all left by which to live: for the "great glory" was the source of his hopes, even though, conjoined with his helplessness (the *king must*), it was the ground of his suffering. The sending for the mirror is a movement towards asking the question "What am I like now I have given everything away?" (see IV. i. 266–7), but has behind it, perhaps, the question "Am I anything at all?" The first question is a move towards self-knowledge, and even repentance:

> I'll read enough
> When I do see the very book indeed
> Where all my sins are writ, and that's myself.

This is but faintly hinted at (and again at V. v. 47–9)[10] But the thought of the mirror is a close neighbour to the thought of annihilation:

> O that I were a mockery king of snow,
> Standing before the sun of Bolingbroke,
> To melt myself away in water-drops!

When the mirror lies to him about his inward condition, he smashes it.[11] He does this, perhaps, simply because of the analogy between its behaviour and that of his flattering followers, and thereby repudiates them and his own folly when he encouraged them in the past. But the smashing is also an act of self-destructive violence, for he has destroyed the image of the face with which he must henceforth live in as manly a fashion as he can:

---

for works (*specula*) of moral instruction (*Mirror for Magistrates* etc.), which is also very common; on this see E. Curtius, *European Literature and the Latin Middle Ages* (London, 1953), p. 336, L. B. Campbell, op. cit., pp. 107–8, M. Doran, *Endeavors of Art* (Madison, 1954), p. 72, R. Bradley, "Speculum Backgrounds in Medieval Literature," *Speculum*, XXIX (1954), 100–15, and cf. *Caes.*, I. iii. 55–8. Shakespeare may have been conscious of both these connotations of the mirror here.

[10] Cf. V. i. 24–5. Dr. Johnson thought that Richard's self-reformation was radical: "In his prosperity we saw him imperious and oppressive, but in his distress he is wise, patient and pious"; cf. Stopford Brooke, *On Ten Plays of Shakespeare* (London, 1905), pp. 97–8.

[11] For a discussion of the light thrown by the references to music in v. v. on Richard's inward condition, see L. Spitzer, "Classical and Christian Ideas of World Harmony," *Traditio* III (1945), 335.

> A brittle glory shineth in this face;
> As brittle as the glory is the face,
> For there it is, crack'd in an hundred shivers.
> Mark, silent king, the moral of this sport—
> How soon my sorrow hath destroy'd my face.

Repudiation of the past self may also be a mere destruction of the self, unless the penitent has the power to contrive a new being. There is no sign that Richard possesses this power. In the prison soliloquy he can picture himself only as something less than a man, an automaton, the Jack of the clock that moves as Bolingbroke bids (V. v. 50–60), or at best his beast of burden (V. v. 92–3). If Richard did ask himself the question "Am I, unkinged, anything?" the answer came back "Nothing at all":

> Then am I king'd again, and by and by
> Think that I am unking'd again by Bolingbroke,
> And straight am nothing.

This is only the confirmation of a truth recognized by sixteenth-century statists: the balm cannot be washed off; the anointed cannot become a man who lives "with bread like you"; for the mark of his divinity is in the bone, and he must either rule or die. Richard's actual death is courageous, or perhaps perfunctory, but it does not alter this.

The play, then, is not simply about a weak but legitimate monarch out-generalled by an able usurper. By showing us this subject in terms of Richard's suffering, Shakespeare adds a further dimension; and extends this beyond the mere pathos of a spectacular fall from glory to dishonour. Shakespeare seems to have used all the skill then at his command to give voice to the inwardness of his protagonist and to show him alive and exciting within the area of his peculiarly exact and individual tragic dilemma: the king who must. As Hazlitt said, "the part of Richard himself gives the chief interest to the play," and with it all the more important problems of its interpretation connect.

"Up, Cousin, Up;
Your Heart Is Up, I Know"

by Brents Stirling

[In III, ii] Shakespeare's inventiveness should be stressed; to the Chronicle version of Richard's misfortune he adds the king's embracing of deposition far in advance of demand or suggestion,[1] and in so doing casts him in a self-made martyr's role. The Flint Castle scene (III. iii) is thus inevitable; figuratively, Richard will depose himself in an agony of play-acting before the unsentimental Bolingbroke.

The outcome at Flint, however, will be unexpected. Not the realist but the sentimentalist will call the turn, and here Shakespeare will answer ironically our question: *when* did Bolingbroke, after all his protests to the contrary, decide to seize the crown? One point of the play, it will appear, is that this question has no point.

In a literal reading, Bolingbroke makes no decision prior to Act IV, and there he is scarcely more than at hand to take the throne. This is subject to several interpretations. First, we might decide that prior to the deposition scene there is no stage at which the deviousness of Bolingbroke becomes clear, and that there are obvious lacunae between his early disclaimers of ambition and his sudden coronation in Act IV. In that event *Richard II* is an inferior play, and the fact that Henry's coronation is also sudden in the chronicles does not make it better. Or, secondly, we might conclude that Elizabethan audiences had heard of Bolingbroke's wish to be king,[2] and that a dramatist of

[1] See Boswell-Stone, *Shakespeare's Holinshed* (London, 1896). Holinshed exhibits Richard in an early state of despair, but with no preconception of dethronement (p. 106), and in a mood of willingness to abdicate after arrival in London (p. 113). Shakespeare, however, presents a king determined to abdicate as early as the landing in Wales (III. ii), before Richard has even encountered Bolingbroke; and he continues to portray him in this mood from there onward.

[2] Samuel Daniel indicates that in Shakespeare's time Bolingbroke's motives were commonly viewed as suspect. He develops the subject at some length (*Civil Wars*, Book I, stanzas 87–99) and concludes that, in charity, judgment should be suspended.

the time did not need to explain it. This could scarcely be denied, but the play, at least to us, would still be the worse for it. Nor, in spite of occasional statements to the contrary, is it Shakespeare's custom to allow major characterization to rest upon history which is external to the play. A third explanation of our "indecisive" Bolingbroke would be that opportunism, of which he becomes the living symbol, is essentially a tacit vice: that although the opportunist is vaguely aware of the ends to which his means commit him, he relies upon events, not upon declarations, to clarify his purposes. On the basis of the scene at Flint and of two prominent episodes which follow it, I believe that the interpretation just expressed is the one which fits the Henry Bolingbroke of Shakespeare's play.

By the time the Flint scene opens we are aware of Richard's impulses toward virtual abdication, but Bolingbroke has never exceeded his demands for simple restitution of rank and estate. Nor have his followers done so. True, York has told him that his very appearance in arms is treason, but Bolingbroke's rejoinder to this has been both disarming and apparently genuine. At the Castle, however, dramatic suggestion begins to take shape. As Henry's followers hold council, Northumberland lets slip the name "Richard" unaccompanied by the title of King. York retorts that such brevity once would have seen him shortened by a head's length. Bolingbroke intercedes: "Mistake not, uncle, further than you should." To which York answers: "Take not, cousin, further than you should." This suggestive colloquy is followed by Bolingbroke's characteristic statement of honest intention: "Go to . . . the castle . . . and thus deliver: Henry Bolingbroke/ On both his knees does kiss King Richard's hand/ And sends allegiance and true faith of heart/ To his most royal person." He will lay down his arms if his lands are restored and his banishment repealed. If not, war is the alternative. With dramatic significance, however, Northumberland, who bears this message from a Bolingbroke "on both his knees," fails himself to kneel before Richard and thus becomes again the medium of suggestive disclosure. Richard, in a rage, sends word back to Henry that "ere the crown he looks for live in peace,/ Ten thousand bloody crowns of mothers' sons" shall be the price in slaughter. Northumberland's rejoinder is a yet more pious assertion of Bolingbroke's limited aims: "The King of heaven forbid our lord the King/ Should so with civil and uncivil arms/ Be rush'd upon! Thy thrice noble cousin/ Harry Bolingbroke . . . swears . . . his coming hath no further scope/ Than for his lineal royalties."

Richard's response is to grant the demands, to render a wish in soliloquy that he be buried where his subjects "may hourly trample on their sovereign's head," and, when summoned to the "base court," to make it a further symbol of the rebels' duplicity, to cry out that down, down he comes "like glist'ring Phaethon,/ Wanting the manage of unruly jades." He enters the lowly court, and the scene concludes with a wonderful mummery of sovereignty, each participant speaking as a subject to his king.

> *Bolingbroke.* Stand all apart,
> And show fair duty to His Majesty. [*He kneels down.*]
> My gracious lord—
> *K. Richard.* Fair Cousin, you debase your princely knee
> To make the base earth proud with kissing it.
> Me rather had my heart might feel your love
> Than my unpleas'd eye see your courtesy.
> Up, cousin, up. Your heart is up, I know,
> Thus high at least, although your knee be low.
> *Bolingbroke.* My gracious lord, I come but for mine own.
> *K. Richard.* Your own is yours, and I am yours, and all.
> *Bolingbroke.* So far be mine, my most redoubted lord,
> As my true service shall deserve your love.
> *K. Richard.* Well you deserve. They well deserve to have
> That know the strong'st and surest way to get. . . .
> Cousin, I am too young to be your father,
> Though you are old enough to be my heir.
> What you will have, I'll give, and willing too;
> For do we must what force will have us do.
> Set on toward London, cousin, is it so?
> *Bolingbroke.* Yea, my good lord.
> *K. Richard.* Then I must not say no.

There is no question of what "London" means. It is dethronement for Richard and coronation for Bolingbroke, an implication which is plain enough here but which Shakespeare underscores in the next scene where the Gardener, asked by the Queen, "Why dost thou say King Richard is deposed?" concludes his answer with "Post you to London, and you will find it so." At Flint, Bolingbroke's reply to Richard, "Yea, my good lord," is the aptly timed climax of the episode, and of the play. With this oblique admission, coming with great effect immediately after his statement of loyalty and subjection, Henry's purposes become clear, and the significant fact is that not he but Richard has phrased his intent. The king's single line, "Set on toward London, cousin, is it so?" is the ironic instrument for exposing a long course of equivocation which the rebels seem to have concealed even from themselves.[3] And in fact Bolingbroke is still trying to conceal it; his short

---

[3] Self-delusion on Bolingbroke's part is a trait clearly suggested by Daniel in his enigmatic passage on Henry's motives (*Civil Wars,* Book I, stanzas 90–91). I men-

answer is the minimum assertion of his motives, an opportunist's spurious appeal to what "must be" in order to avoid a statement of purpose.

This turn in the play rests upon skillful fusion of three elements—plot construction, disclosure of political moral, and characterization, all of which show parallel irony. In plot unfoldment, the end of the Flint scene is the point of climax at which Henry's true purpose is revealed. But the climax is also a studied anticlimax, for the rebels advance upon Flint Castle only, as it were, to find it abandoned and with the words, "Come to London," written upon the walls. They, and the audience, had expected not quiet exposure of their aims (the actual climax) but dramatic opportunity for constitutional manifestoes.

As for disclosure of political doctrine, it is during the encounter at Flint that the rebels achieve their most eloquent statement of legality in seeking only a subject's claim to justice from his king. But the luxury of that pretense vanishes at the end of the scene, again with the word "London." It becomes suddenly apparent that York's previous judgment was sound, that Bolingbroke's use of force to gain just concessions from his sovereign has committed him to the destruction of sovereignty.

The third factor here is characterization which greatly enhances the complex of ironies. Shakespeare's prior establishment of Bolingbroke's realism, self-containment, and resourcefulness, along with Richard's romantic defeatism, near-hysteria, and pathetic reliance upon others, has furnished a decided pattern for the meeting of the two at Flint. Bolingbroke (with Northumberland) fulfills previously set notes of stability and restraint; Richard repeats the performance he had enacted before his own followers in the preceding scene, and reminds us of a familiar epigram about the protagonist who is spectator at his own tragedy. Full portraiture of Bolingbroke and Richard, both before and during the Castle episode, thus prepares for the paradoxical ending of the scene. There, with Richard's knowing reference to London and Bolingbroke's one-line reply, the shift in characterization materializes. The unstable Richard, who had fled from facts through every

---

tion this only to show that such an interpretation was made at the time *Richard II* was written. The concluding lines of stanza 91 are:

> Men do not know what then themselves will be
> When-as, more than themselves, themselves they see.

For an additional reference to Daniel, as well as for a denial that Bolingbroke is a conscious schemer, see J. Dover Wilson's edition of *Richard II* (Cambridge, 1939), pp. xx and xxi. Mr. Wilson briefly describes Bolingbroke as an opportunist led by Fortune.

form of emotional exaggeration, now drops his sentimental role and points to reality with quiet wit and candor; the plain-dealing Boling-broke who had offered his demands with such consistency and seeming honesty, now admits his sham of rebellion which was to stop short of rebellion.

The end of Act III, scene iii, is thus pivotal. At this point of mul-tiple effect Bolingbroke's ambiguity is revealed, and it now engages Shakespeare's attention in a pair of episodes which will complete Henry's portrait; the ambiguity will be presented twice again by means of the same dramatic method.

The first of these cumulative parallels to the Flint scene occurs in IV. i (the deposition). Here Richard is again confronted by the rebels, and again he is by turns both defiant and submissive; his sentimental display is likewise in dramatic contrast with Henry's simplicity, for-bearance, and directness. And as before, the paradox comes in the clos-ing lines:

> *K. Richard.* I'll beg one boon,
>   And then be gone and trouble you no more.
>   Shall I obtain it?
> *Bolingbroke.* Name it, fair Cousin.
> *K. Richard.* "Fair Cousin"? I am greater than a king.
>   For when I was a king, my flatterers
>   Were then but subjects. Being now a subject,
>   I have a King here to my flatterer.
>   Being so great, I have no need to beg.
> *Bolingbroke.* Yet ask.
> *K. Richard.* And shall I have?
> *Bolingbroke.* You shall.
> *K. Richard.* Then give me leave to go.
> *Bolingbroke.* Whither?
> *K. Richard.* Whither you will, so I were from your sights.
> *Bolingbroke.* Go, some of you convey him to the Tower.

Just as "London" meant deposition at the end of III. iii, so here at the end of IV. i the Tower means imprisonment and ultimate death. Again Richard, who has run his course of theatrical emotion, becomes pointedly realistic: again Bolingbroke, who has exhibited every sign of gracious honesty, reveals duplicity in a concluding line.

The third and final step in Henry's portrayal is analogous in all essentials to the two scenes we have examined. The fact that Shake-speare here drew upon the Chronicles might imply that he found there a suggestion of the shifting taciturnity which Bolingbroke shows in all three episodes. Piers of Exton, in V. iv, ponders something he has heard. "Have I no friend will rid me of this living fear?" Was not that what the new king said? And did he not repeat it as he "wishtly look'd on me"? It is enough; Exton promptly murders Richard and returns with the body. Henry's lines which conclude the play are well known; he admits desiring Richard's death but disowns Exton's act and pledges expiation in a voyage to the Holy Land.

Three times—at the end of III. iii, at the end of the deposition scene, and in the Exton scenes at the end of the play—Henry has taken, if it may be so called, a decisive step. Each time the move he has made has been embodied in a terse statement, and each time someone else has either evoked it from him or stated its implications for him. Never in sixteenth-century drama were motives disclosed with such economy and understatement. The Elizabethan stage character with a moral contradiction usually explains his flaw before, during, and after the event—and at length. Until the short choric "confession" at the very end of the play, Bolingbroke, however, shows his deviousness in one-line admissions spaced at telling intervals and occurring in contexts which are effectively similar.

And as each of these admissions marks a step in characterization, it indicates a critical stage of plot development: the conflict of forces is resolved with the line on London concluding the Flint Castle scene, for there Richard and Henry reach mutual understanding on the dethronement issue; the falling action becomes defined with the line near the end of the deposition scene which sends Richard to the Tower; the catastrophe is begun by the line to Exton which sends him to death.

Finally, at each of these three points the meaning implicit in the play shows a new clarity. With the reference to London at Flint it becomes apparent that a "constitutional" show of force against sovereignty leads to the deposition of sovereignty; with the dispatching of Richard to the Tower it appears that deposition of sovereignty requires degradation of the sovereign; and with Henry's line to Exton it becomes plain that murder of sovereignty must be the final outcome.[4]

From his first history to his last tragedy Shakespeare excelled in a poet's expression of Tudor political dogma. But to say this is not enough, for as early as *Richard II* he combined his poet's talent with

---

[4] The Chronicle accounts of Richard's latter days do not provide a suggestion of these cumulative steps. As usual, a play-source comparison emphasizes Shakespeare's artistry both in structure and motivation. Daniel (*Civil Wars*, Books I and II) likewise fails to present Bolingbroke's opportunistic conduct in the telling manner of Shakespeare. He does amply suggest the possibility of "unconscious" drift toward usurpation but in no way dramatizes this action in successive, cumulative disclosure. Daniel is not to be regarded with certainty as a source of Shakespeare; it is possible that similarities between the *Civil Wars* and *Richard II* are to be accounted for by Daniel having seen the play. In any event, a comparison of Shakespeare and Daniel is revealing.

another difficult art. In this play doctrine, plot, and characterization unfold integrally. With our debt to the English and American revolutions we cannot admire the doctrine, but we can recognize in *Richard II* a stage of Shakespeare's development at which morality and artistry become functionally inseparable.

The Kings

by Jan Kott

What, do you tremble? Are you all afraid?
Alas, I blame you not, for you are mortal . . .

(*Richard III*, I, 2)

A careful reading of the list of characters in *Richard III* is enough
to show what sort of historical material Shakespeare used in order to
illustrate facts relating to his own period and to fill the stage with his
real contemporaries. Here, in one of his earliest plays—or rather in its
historical raw material—one can already see the outline of all the later
great tragedies: of *Hamlet, Macbeth* and *King Lear.* If one wishes to
interpret Shakespeare's world as the real world, one should start the
reading of the plays with the Histories, and in particular, with
Richard II and *Richard III.* . . .

Shakespeare is like the world, or life itself. Every historical period
finds in him what it is looking for and what it wants to see. A reader or
spectator in the mid-twentieth century interprets *Richard III* through
his own experiences. He cannot do otherwise. And that is why he is not
terrified—or rather, not amazed—at Shakespeare's cruelty. He views
the struggle for power and mutual slaughter of the characters far more
calmly than did many generations of spectators and critics in the nine-
teenth century. More calmly, or, at any rate, more rationally. Cruel
death, suffered by most *dramatis personae,* is not regarded today as
an aesthetic necessity, or as an essential rule in tragedy in order to
produce *catharsis,* or even as a specific characteristic of Shakespeare's
genius. Violent deaths of the principal characters are now regarded
rather as an historical necessity, or as something altogether natural.
Even in *Titus Andronicus,* written, or rewritten, by Shakespeare probably in the same year as *King Richard III,* modern audiences see much
more than the ludicrous and grotesque accumulation of needless hor-

"The Kings." From Jan Kott, Shakespeare Our Contemporary, *trans. Boleslaw
Taborski. Copyright © 1964 by Panstwowe Wydawnictwo Naukowe. Copyright ©
1964, 1965, 1966 by Doubleday & Company, Inc. Copyright © 1966 by Methuen &
Company, Ltd. Reprinted by permission of the publishers.*

rors which nineteenth-century critics found in it. And when *Titus Andronicus* received a production like that by Peter Brook, today's audiences were ready to applaud the general slaughter in act five no less enthusiastically than Elizabethan coppersmiths, tailors, butchers and soldiers had done. In those days the play was one of the greatest theatrical successes. By discovering in Shakespeare's plays problems that are relevant to our own time, modern audiences often, unexpectedly, find themselves near to the Elizabethans; or at least are in the position to understand them well. This is particularly true of the Histories.

Shakespeare's History plays take their titles from the names of kings: *King John, King Richard II, Henry IV, Henry V, Henry VI, Richard III (King Henry VIII*, a work partly written by Shakespeare towards the close of his literary activities, belongs to the History plays solely in a formal sense). Apart from *King John*, which deals with events at the turn of the thirteenth century, Shakespeare's Histories deal with the struggle for the English crown that went on from the close of the fourteenth to the end of the fifteenth century. They constitute an historical epic covering over a hundred years and divided into long chapters corresponding to reigns. But when we read these chapters chronologically, following the sequence of reigns, we are struck by the thought that for Shakespeare history stands still. Every chapter opens and closes at the same point. In every one of these plays history turns full circle, returning to the point of departure. These recurring and unchanging circles described by history are the successive kings' reigns.

Each of these great historical tragedies begins with a struggle for the throne, or for its consolidation. Each ends with the monarch's death and a new coronation. In each of the Histories the legitimate ruler drags behind him a long chain of crimes. He has rejected the feudal lords who helped him to reach for the crown; he murders, first, his enemies, then his former allies; he executes possible successors and pretenders to the crown. But he has not been able to execute them all. From banishment a young prince returns—the son, grandson, or brother of those murdered—to defend the violated law. The rejected lords gather round him, he personifies the hope for a new order and justice. But every step to power continues to be marked by murder, violence, treachery. And so, when the new prince finds himself near the throne, he drags behind him a chain of crimes as long as that of the until now legitimate ruler. When he assumes the crown, he will be just as hated as his predecessor. He has killed enemies, now he will kill former allies. And a new pretender appears in the name of violated justice. The wheel has turned full circle. A new chapter opens. A new historical tragedy:

Then thus:
Edward the Third, my lords, had seven sons:
The first, Edward the Black Prince, Prince of Wales;
The second, William of Hatfield; and the third,
Lionel Duke of Clarence; next to whom
Was John of Gaunt, the Duke of Lancaster;
The fifth was Edmund Langley, Duke of York;
The sixth was Thomas of Woodstock, Duke of Gloucester;
William of Windsor was the seventh and last.
Edward the Black Prince died before his father
And left behind him Richard, his only son,
Who after Edward the Third's death reign'd as king
Till Henry Bolingbroke, Duke of Lancaster,
The eldest son and heir of John of Gaunt,
Crown'd by the name of Henry the Fourth,
Seiz'd on the realm, depos'd the rightful king,
Sent his poor queen to France, from whence she came,
And him to Pomfret, where, as all you know,
Harmless Richard was murthered traitorously.

                                        (2 *Henry VI*, II, 2)

This scheme of things is not, of course, marked with equally clear-cut outline in all Shakespeare's Histories. It is clearest in *King John* and in the two masterpieces of historical tragedy, *Richard II* and *Richard III*. It is least clear in *Henry V*, an idealized and patriotic play which depicts a struggle with an enemy from without. But in Shakespeare's plays the struggle for power is always stripped of all mythology, shown in its "pure state." It is a struggle for the crown, between people who have a name, a title and power.

In the Middle Ages the clearest image of wealth was a bag full of golden pieces. Each of them could be weighed in hand. For many centuries wealth meant fields, meadows and woods, flocks of sheep, a castle and villages. Later a ship loaded with pepper, or cloves, or big granaries filled with sacks of wheat, cellars full of wines, stores along the Thames emitting a sour smell of leather and the choking dust of cotton. Riches could be seen, handled and smelt. It was only later that they dematerialized, became a symbol, something abstract. Wealth ceased to be a concrete thing and became a slip of paper with writing on it. Those changes were described by Karl Marx in *Das Kapital*.

In a similar fashion power was dematerialized, or rather, disembodied. It ceased to have a name. It became something abstract and mythological, almost a pure idea. But for Shakespeare power has names, eyes, mouth and hands. It is a relentless struggle of living people who sit together at one table.

> For God's sake let us sit upon the ground
> And tell sad stories of the death of kings!
> How some have been depos'd, some slain in war,
> Some haunted by the ghosts they have depos'd,
> Some poisoned by their wives, some sleeping kill'd—
> All murthered; . . .   (*Richard II*, III, 2)

For Shakespeare the crown is the image of power. It is heavy. It can be handled, torn off a dying king's head, and put on one's own. Then one becomes a king. Only then. But one must wait till the king is dead, or else precipitate his death.

> He cannot live, I hope, and must not die
> Till George be pack'd with posthorse up to heaven.
> I'll in, to urge his hatred more to Clarence
> With lies well steel'd with weighty arguments;
>
> Which done, God take King Edward to his mercy
> And leave the world for me to bustle in!
>   (*Richard III*, I, 1)

In each of the Histories there are four or five men who look into the eyes of the dying monarch, watch his trembling hands. They have already laid a plot, brought their loyal troops to the capital, communicated with their vassals. They have given orders to hired assassins; the stony Tower awaits new prisoners. There are four or five men, but only one of them may remain alive. Each of them has a different name and title. Each has a different face. One is cunning, another brave; the third is cruel, the fourth—a cynic. They are living people, for Shakespeare was a great writer. We remember their faces. But when we finish reading one chapter and begin to read the next one, when we read the Histories in their entirety, the faces of kings and usurpers become blurred, one after the other.

Even their names are the same. There is always a Richard, an Edward and a Henry. They have the same titles. There is a Duke of York, a Prince of Wales, a Duke of Clarence. In the different plays different people are brave, or cruel, or cunning. But the drama that is being played out between them is always the same. And in every tragedy the same cry, uttered by mothers of the murdered kings, is repeated:

> *Queen Margaret.* I had an Edward, till a Richard kill'd him;
>   I had a Harry, till a Richard kill'd him:
>   Thou hadst an Edward, till a Richard kill'd him;
>   Thou hadst a Richard, till a Richard kill'd him.
> *Duchess of York.* I had a Richard too, and thou didst kill him;
>   I had a Rutland too, thou holp'st to kill him.
> *Queen Margaret.* Thy Edward he is dead, that kill'd my Edward;

Thy other Edward dead, to quit my Edward;
Young York he is but boot, because both they
Match'd not the high perfection of my loss.
Thy Clarence he is dead that stabb'd my Edward,
And the beholders of this frantic play,
Th' adulterate Hastings, Rivers, Vaughan, Grey,
Untimely smother'd in their dusky graves.

                                        (*Richard III*, IV, 4)

Emanating from the features of individual kings and usurpers in
Shakespeare's History plays, there gradually emerges the image of
history itself. The image of the Grand Mechanism. Every successive
chapter, every great Shakespearean act is merely a repetition:

The flattering index of a direful pageant,
One heav'd a-high to be hurl'd down below, . . .
                                        (*Richard III*, IV, 4)

It is this image of history, repeated many times by Shakespeare, that
forces itself on us in a most powerful manner. Feudal history is like a
great staircase on which there treads a constant procession of kings.
Every step upwards is marked by murder, perfidy, treachery. Every
step brings the throne nearer. Another step and the crown will fall.
One will soon be able to snatch it.

                                . . . That is a step
On which I must fall down, or else o'erleap, . . .
                                        (*Macbeth*, I, 4)

From the highest step there is only a leap into the abyss. The mon-
archs change. But all of them—good and bad, brave and cowardly,
vile and noble, naive and cynical—tread on the steps that are always
the same.

Was this how Shakespeare conceived the tragedy of history in his
first, youthful period that has light-heartedly been called "optimistic"?
Or was he, perhaps, an adherent of absolute monarchy and used the
bloody stuff of fifteenth-century history to shock the audience by his
spectacle of feudal struggles and England's internal disruption? Or did
he write about his own times? Perhaps *Hamlet* is not so far removed
from the two *Richard* plays? On what experiences did he draw? Was
he a moralist, or did he describe the world he knew or foresaw, without illusions, without contempt, but also without indignation? Let us
try to interpret *Richard II* and *Richard III* as best we can.

Let us begin by tracing the working of the Grand Mechanism as
Shakespeare shows it in his theatre. On the proscenium two armies

fight each other. The tiny inner stage is turned into the House of Commons, or the King's chamber. On the balcony the King appears, surrounded by bishops. Trumpets are blown: the proscenium is now the Tower courtyard where the imprisoned princes are being led under guard. The inner stage has been turned into a cell. The successor to the throne cannot sleep, tormented by thoughts of violence. Now the door opens, and hired assassins enter with daggers in their hands. A moment later the proscenium is a London street at night: frightened townsmen hurry past talking politics. Trumpets again: the new monarch has made his appearance on the balcony.

Let us begin with the great abdication scene in *Richard II,* the scene omitted in all editions published in Queen Elizabeth's lifetime. It revealed the working of the Grand Mechanism too brutally: the very moment when power was changing hands. Authority comes either from God, or from the people. A flash of the sword, the tramping of the guards; applause of intimidated noblemen; a shout from the forcibly gathered crowd; and behold: the new authority, too, comes from God, or from the will of the people.

Henry Bolingbroke, later King Henry IV, has returned from exile, landed with an army and captured Richard II, deserted by his vassals. The coup d'état has been accomplished. It has yet to be legalized. The former King still lives.

> Fetch hither Richard, that in common view
> He may surrender. So we shall proceed
> Without suspicion.

Richard enters under guard, deprived of his royal robes. Following him are noblemen carrying royal insignia. The scene takes place in the House of Lords. The proscenium represents Westminster Hall, which has been reconstructed by Richard and given its famous oak ceiling. He has been brought beneath it only once, in order to abdicate.

Says the King, deprived of his crown:

> Alack, why am I sent for to a king
> Before I have shook off the regal thoughts
> Wherewith I reign'd? I hardly yet have learn'd
> To insinuate, flatter, bow, and bend my limbs.
> Give sorrow leave awhile to tutor me
> To this submission. Yet I well remember
> The favours of these men. Were they not mine?
> Did they not sometime cry 'All hail!' to me?

But he is not allowed to speak for long. He is handed the crown to hold it for a moment and give it to Henry. Give it of his own free will. He has already renounced his power, rents and revenues. He has

cancelled his decrees and statutes. What else can they want of him?
"What more remains?" Shakespeare knew:

> . . . No more, but that you read
> These accusations and these grievous crimes
> Committed by your person and your followers
> Against the state and profit of this land,
> That, by confessing them, the souls of men
> May deem that you are worthily depos'd.

Says the King, deprived of his crown:

> Must I do so? and must I ravel out
> My weav'd-up folly? Gentle Northumberland,
> If thy offences were upon record,
> Would it not shame thee in so fair a troop
> To read a lecture of them?

But again he is not allowed to speak for long. The act of dethronement has to be completed quickly and absolutely. The King's royal
majesty must be extinguished. The new King is waiting. If the former
King is not a traitor, then the new one is a usurper. One can well
understand Queen Elizabeth's censors:

> *Northumberland.* My lord, dispatch. Read o'er these articles.
> *King Richard.* Mine eyes are full of tears; I cannot see.
> And yet salt water blinds them not so much
> But they can see a sort of traitors here.
> Nay, if I turn mine eyes upon myself,
> I find myself a traitor with the rest;
> For I have given here my soul's consent
> To undeck the pompous body of a king; . . .

When dramatizing history, Shakespeare first and foremost condenses
it. For history itself is more dramatic than the particular dramas of
John, the Henrys and the Richards. The greatest drama consists in
the working of the Grand Mechanism. Shakespeare can contain years
in a month, months in a day, in one great scene, in three or four
speeches which comprise the very essence of history.

Here is the grand finale of any dethronement:

> *King Richard.* Then give me leave to go.
> *Bolingbroke.* Whither?
> *King Richard.* Whither you will, so I were from your sights.
> *Bolingbroke.* Go some of you, convey him to the Tower.

> On Wednesay next we solemnly set down
> Our coronation. Lords, prepare yourselves.
>
> *(Richard II, IV, 1)*

It is nearly the end. There is just one more act to come. The last one. But this act will at the same time be the first act of a new tragedy. It will have a new title, of course: *Henry IV*. In *Richard II* Bolingbroke was a "positive hero"; an avenger. He defended violated law and justice. But in his own tragedy he can only play the part of Richard II. The cycle has been completed. The cycle is beginning again. Bolingbroke has mounted half way up the grand staircase of history. He has been crowned; he is reigning. Dressed in the royal robes, he is awaiting the dignitaries of the realm at Windsor Castle. They duly arrive.

> *Northumberland.* First, to thy sacred state wish I all happiness.
> The next news is, I have to London sent
> The heads of Oxford, Salisbury, Blunt, and Kent.
>
> *Bolingbroke.* We thank thee, gentle Percy, for thy pains
> And to thy worth will add right worthy gains.
> *(Enter* Fitzwater)
> *Fitzwater.* My lord, I have from Oxford sent to London
> The heads of Brocas and Sir Bennet Seely,
> Two of the dangerous consorted traitors
> That sought at Oxford thy dire overthrow.
> *Bolingbroke.* Thy pains, Fitzwater, shall not be forgot.
> Right noble is thy merit, well I wot.   *(Richard II, V, 6)*

The most terrifying thing about this scene is its natural matter-of-factness. As if nothing has happened. As if everything went according to the natural order of things. A new reign has begun: six heads are being sent to the capital for the new King. But Shakespeare cannot end a tragedy in this way. A shock is needed. The working of the Grand Mechanism has to be high-lighted by a flash of awareness. Just one; but it is a flash of genius. The new King is waiting for one more head; the most important one. He has commanded his most trusted follower to commit the murder. Commanded—this is too simple a word. Kings do not order assassination; they only allow it, in such a way that they shall not know about it themselves. But let us go back to Shakespeare's own words. For this is one of those great scenes that history will repeat; scenes that have been written once and for all. There is everything in them: the mechanism of the human heart, and the mechanism of power; there is fear, flattery, and "the system." In this scene the King does not take part, and no name is mentioned. There are only the King's words, and their double echo. This is one of the scenes in which Shakespeare is truer to life than life itself.

> *Exton.* Didst thou not mark the King, what words he spake?
> 'Have I no friend will rid me of this living fear?'
> Was it not so?
> *Servant.*   These were his very words.
> *Exton.* 'Have I no friend?' quoth he. He spake it twice
> And urg'd it twice together, did he not?
> *Servant.* He did.   (*Richard II*, V, 4)

And now, in the very last scene of *Richard II*, this most faithful of loyal subjects enters, with servants carrying a coffin:

> Great King, within this coffin I present
> Thy buried fear. Herein all breathless lies
> The mightiest of thy greatest enemies,
> Richard of Bordeaux, by me hither brought.
>   (*Richard II*, V, 6)

It is now that a flash of genius manifests itself. Let us omit the King's reply: it is pedestrian. He will banish Exton, order a state funeral for Richard with himself as the chief mourner. All this is still within the bounds of the Grand Mechanism, described drily, as in a medieval chronicle. But the King lets slip a sentence that foreshadows the problems of *Hamlet*. And, indeed, *Hamlet* must only be interpreted in the light of the two *Richard* plays. This sentence expresses a sudden fear of the world and its cruel mechanism, from which there is no escape, but which one cannot accept. For there are no bad kings, or good kings; kings are only kings. Or let us put it in modern terms: there is only the king's situation, and the system. This situation leaves no room for freedom of choice. At the end of the tragedy the King speaks a sentence that might be spoken by Hamlet:

> They love not poison that do poison need, . . .
>   (*Richard II*, V, 6)

In Shakespeare's world there is a contradiction between the order of action and the moral order. This contradiction is human fate. One cannot get away from it.

The Henriad: Shakespeare's Major
History Plays

by Alvin B. Kernan

Taken together, Shakespeare's four major history plays, *Richard II*, *1 Henry IV*, *2 Henry IV*, and *Henry V* constitute an epic, *The Henriad*. Obviously these four plays are not an epic in the usual sense—there is no evidence that Shakespeare planned them as a unit—but they do have remarkable coherence and they possess that quality which in our time we take to be the chief characteristic of epic: a large-scale, heroic action, involving many men and many activities, tracing the movement of a nation or people through violent change from one condition to another. In *The Iliad* that action involves the wrath of Achilles and the misfortunes which it brought to the Achaeans before Troy. In *The Aeneid* the action is the transferal of the Empire of Troy to Latium. And in *Paradise Lost* the action is man's first disobedience and the fruit of that forbidden tree.

In *The Henriad,* the action is the passage from the England of Richard II to the England of Henry V. This dynastic shift serves as the supporting framework for a great many cultural and psychological transitions which run parallel to the main action, giving it body and meaning. In historical terms the movement from the world of Richard II to that of Henry V is the passage from the Middle Ages to the Renaissance and the modern world. In political and social terms it is a movement from feudalism and hierarchy to the national state and individualism. In psychological terms it is a passage from a situation in which man knows with certainty who he is to an existential condition in which any identity is only a temporary role. In spatial and temporal terms it is a movement from a closed world to an infinite universe. In mythical terms the passage is from a garden world to a fallen world. In the most summary terms it is a movement from ceremony and ritual to history:

"The Henriad: Shakespeare's Major History Plays" by Alvin B. Kernan. First published in a shorter form in The Yale Review, *59, no. 1 (Fall, 1969): 3-32. Copyright © 1969 by Yale University. Reprinted by permission of* The Yale Review *and the author.*

The Renaissance was a moment when educated men were modifying a ceremonial conception of human life to create a historical conception. The ceremonial view, which assumed that names and meanings are fixed and final, expressed experience as pageant and ritual—pageant where the right names could march in proper order, or ritual where names could be changed in the right, the proper way. The historical view expresses life as drama. People in drama are not identical with their names, for they gain and lose their names, their status and meaning—and not by settled ritual: the gaining and losing of names, of meaning, is beyond the control of any set ritual sequence. . . . The people in [Shakespeare's] plays try to organize their lives by pageant and ritual, but the plays are dramatic precisely because the effort fails.[1]

It is by means of ceremony and ritual that the old kingdom is presented in the beginning of *The Henriad*. *Richard II* opens on a scene in which two furious peers, Mowbray and Hereford, confront and accuse one another of treason before their legitimate king. The place of judgment is the court itself, with all its ceremonial forms and symbols: crowns, trumpets, thrones, ranked retainers, robes of state and heraldic arms. This court, in its traditional setting with its ancient emblems and established procedures, repeats the pattern of innumerable former assemblies convoked for the same purpose, to absorb and reorder once again the disorderly elements in man and society.

When this ritual attempt fails, an even more solemn ritual is ordered, trial by combat. The ceremonial elements in I. iii are heavily emphasized: the combatant knights enter in the proper manner and take their assigned places in the lists. They make the expected speeches, and the marshal of the lists puts the formulaic questions to them.

> *The trumpets sound. Enter* Bolingbroke, Duke of Hereford, *appellant,* in *armour, and a* Herald.
> *King Richard.* Marshal, ask yonder knight in arms,
>   Both who he is and why he cometh hither
>   Thus plated in habiliments of war;
>   And formally, according to our law,
>   Depose him in the justice of his cause.
> *Marshal.* What is thy name? and wherefore com'st thou hither
>   Before King Richard in his royal lists?
>   Against whom comest thou? and what's thy quarrel?
>   Speak like a true knight, so defend thee heaven!
> *Bolingbroke.* Harry of Hereford, Lancaster, and Derby,

---

[1] C. L. Barber, *Shakespeare's Festive Comedy: A Study of Dramatic Form and Its Relation to Social Custom* (Princeton, 1959), p. 193.

Am I; who ready here do stand in arms
To prove, by God's grace and my body's valour,
In lists on Thomas Mowbray, Duke of Norfolk,
That he is a traitor, foul and dangerous,
To God of heaven, King Richard, and to me.
And as I truly fight, defend me heaven!

(*Richard II*, I. iii. 26–41)

Here, and throughout the early acts of the play, traditional ways of acting and traditional values—the law, the sanctity of a knight's oath, established duty to God and king—reflected in the formulaic phrases, the conventional terms, and the orderly rhythms, control the violent passions, fury, fear, outrage, hatred, the lust for power, at work in Richard's England. The individual is submerged within the role imposed upon him by prescribed ways of thinking, acting, and speaking.

But, even as we admire, this old world is breaking up. The patriarchs of England—the seven sons of Edward II—are, like the twelve sons of Jacob, passing from the land, and with them their world passes. The sense of an ancient, more perfect world, fading from existence into memory is focused in John of Gaunt's comparison of England, as it was only yesterday, to another Eden:

This royal throne of kings, this scept'red isle,
This earth of majesty, this seat of Mars,
This other Eden, demi-paradise,
This fortress built by Nature for herself
Against infection and the hand of war,
This happy breed of men, this little world,
This precious stone set in the silver sea,
Which serves it in the office of a wall,
Or as a moat defensive to a house,
Against the envy of less happier lands;
This blessed plot, this earth, this realm, this England. . . .

(*Richard II*, II. i. 40–50)

By III. iv when the "sea-walled garden" appears again, presided over by a gardener in "old Adam's likeness," it is full of weeds, the flowers choked, the trees unpruned, the hedges in ruin, the herbs eaten by caterpillars, and the great tree in its center dead.

What is passing in the course of *Richard II* is innocence, a sense of living in a golden world, and no one is more innocent than Richard himself. When Bolingbroke begins his rebellion, Richard confidently expects that God himself will send down soldiers to defend him and blast the usurper. The order of nature and the laws of men, he believes, guarantee his kingship:

Not all the water in the rough rude sea
Can wash the balm off from an anointed king;
The breath of worldly men cannot depose
The deputy elected by the Lord.
For every man that Bolingbroke hath press'd
To lift shrewd steel against our golden crown,
God for his Richard hath in heavenly pay
A glorious angel. Then, if angels fight,
Weak men must fall; for heaven still guards the right.
                                             (*Richard II,* III. ii. 54–62)

Richard, here and elsewhere in the play, manifests his belief in the conservative world view which has been variously called "The Great Chain of Being, "The Elizabethan World Picture," and "The Tudor Political Myth." This world view imaged the whole of creation, from God down to the meanest pebble, as being organized hierarchically, as a series of rungs in a ladder or links in a chain. Each category in turn mirrored the systematic arrangement of the whole, and its parts were distributed in descending order of authority, responsibility, and power. To act "naturally," to live in accordance with things as they are, was to accept your assigned place in society, controlled justly by the powers above and controlling justly those below entrusted to your care and authority. When man acted in a disorderly fashion, creating a disturbance within his own "little world" or microcosm, "Nature" quickly acted to right itself: all the other categories of being trembled sympathetically, the ripples spread through all creation, and the great powers began to react to restore order. This world view saw in all areas of life—religion, physics, psychology, government, zoology, and all social organizations—a reflection of the human dream of order, stability, harmony, coherence, and community. Life ideally lived was a dance or music.

Richard takes this great imaginative projection of human values for absolute fact, mistakes metaphor for science, and so believes that God will directly intervene in the coming battle and that the king's appearance in England will cause rebellion to disappear just as the rising of the sun (the "king" of the cosmos) banishes night and darkness. Like a child, he fails to distinguish human desire from actuality and therefore fails to understand that he cannot trust to "Nature" to maintain him as a king, simply because he *is* king. From the outset of the play powerful political and personal forces are at work undermining the social system, making a mockery of ritual and ceremony. Mowbray has been involved in graft and assassination for political purposes. Henry Hereford has been courting popularity with the common people, and he accuses Mowbray of treason knowing that he is innocent. His motive may be to embarrass Richard, who is himself deeply implicated in the murder of his uncle, Duke of Gloucester, the crime of which Mowbray is accused. Richard is violently jealous and suspicious of his cousin Hereford and uses the trial as an occasion for banishing him under the pretense of being merciful. Pressed by the perpetual need for money, Richard sells his right to gather taxes to profiteers. He neglects affairs of state to spend his time reveling with male favorites. Each of these acts indirectly undermines the order which Richard thinks immutable, and when upon John of Gaunt's death he seizes the banished Hereford's lands, he strikes a direct blow, as the Duke of York points out, against the great law of orderly succession on which his kingship rests:

> Take Hereford's rights away, and take from Time
> His charters and his customary rights;
> Let not to-morrow then ensue to-day;
> Be not thyself—for how art thou a king
> But by fair sequence and succession?
> *(Richard II,* II. i. 95–99)

In general, Richard treats his kingdom and subjects in an arbitrary manner, and the play realizes his implication in his own destruction in the scene in which he uncrowns himself, names Bolingbroke his successor, and confesses the sins which brought him down. This is, of course, good political strategy for Bolingbroke, who, like modern dictators, realizes that nothing is so valuable to an uneasy ruler as his victim's public confession and admission of the justice of punishment. But the scene has another function. By uncrowning himself visibly, Richard is repeating and making manifest what he did earlier in the play when he worked so busily and blindly to destroy the values and rituals on which his kingship rested.

In *Paradise Lost* the results of the fall, Adam and Eve's disobedience to God, are immediate and spectacular: the earth tilts and the seasons become intemperate, the animals become vicious and prey on one another and on man, and man himself knows fear, anger, lust, and shame. What Milton presents on the scale of the universe, Shakespeare presents on the scale of the kingdom and the individual. Most immediately, Richard's disorders release a variety of other disorders on all levels of life. Richard having rebelled against the order which made and kept him king, Henry Bolingbroke immediately rebels against Richard. By the end of the play there is already another group of plotters planning to overthrow Henry. Throughout the three succeeding plays political scheming, plotting, raids on the commonwealth, and civil wars never cease. As one group of rebels dies, another group is already forming to take its place, each more desperate

and violent than the last. Henry IV lives out his days facing one revolt after another, and even Henry V, whose reign in some ways is a
restoration of political order, is still forced to deal with treasons
which are "like/ Another fall of man" (*Henry V*, II. ii. 141–42).

As the old political order weakens, simple men like the good old
Duke of York become confused and inept. His duty is, he knows, to
his king; but who is his king? what to do if that duty now conflicts
with other primary duties? The confusion in his mind is reflected in
the confusion in his family. His son, the Duke of Aumerle, intrigues
against the new king, and the Duchess of York tells her husband that
his primary duty lies not to the King but to his own son. But the
anguished York goes to the King to accuse his son of treason. This
civil war within the family eventuates in an absurd scene in which
the King hears York ask him to execute his son, while the Duchess of
York asks the King for mercy and pleads against her own husband.
The most serious matters have become a kind of mad joke. The disorder in York's family expands to the family of Henry, and by the
end of the play we learn that Hal, the Prince of Wales, is already
roistering in a tavern, defying his father, and using his power to
break the law with impunity.

As the old order breaks up, a profound psychological confusion
parallels the political confusion. In that Edenic world which Gaunt
described and Richard destroyed, every man knew who he was. His
religion, his family, his position in society, his assigned place in pro-
cessions large and small, his coat of arms, his traditional duties, and
even his clothing, which was then prescribed by sumptuary laws,
told him who he was and what he should do and even gave him the
formal language in which to express this socially-assigned self. But
once, under the pressures of political necessity and personal desires,
the old system is destroyed, the old identities go with it. Man then
finds himself in the situation which Richard acts out in IV. i, the
deposition scene. Richard is speaking, and when Northumberland attempts to break in with the exclamation "My lord," he responds with
words which reveal how thoroughly shattered is his sense of the
power of his name and the immutability of his identity as Richard
Plantagenet, King of England:

> No lord of thine, thou haught insulting man,
> Nor no man's lord; I have no name, no title—
> No, not that name was given me at the font—
> But 'tis usurp'd. Alack the heavy day,
> That I have worn so many winters out,
> And know not now what name to call myself!
>   (*Richard II*, IV. i. 254–59)

Like the great actor he is, Richard cannot pass the opportunity to
demonstrate visually the lesson he has learned. He calls for a looking
glass, and holding it before his face he muses:

> No deeper wrinkles yet? Hath sorrow struck
> So many blows upon this face of mine
> And made no deeper wounds? O flatt'ring glass,
> Like to my followers in prosperity,
> Thou dost beguile me! Was this face the face
> That every day under his household roof
> Did keep ten thousand men? Was this the face
> That like the sun did make beholders wink?
> Is this the face which fac'd so many follies,
> That was at last out-fac'd by Bolingbroke?
> A brittle glory shineth in this face;
> As brittle as the glory is the face;
> [*He breaks the mirror.*]
>   (*Richard II*, IV. i. 277–88)

Having already discovered that one's name can change rapidly in the
world, Richard now becomes self-conscious, aware that the unchanged
face he views in the glass squares with neither his greatly changed
political condition nor his equally changed inner sense of himself.

Richard is not the first man in this play to discover that he no
longer knows who he is. He has already forced the question of identity on Bolingbroke by banishing him from England and robbing him
of his succession as Duke of Lancaster. Bolingbroke—whose names
change rapidly: Hereford, Bolingbroke, Lancaster, and Henry IV—has
understood the lesson well. Speaking to Bushy and Green, two of
Richard's favorites, the man who had once confidently answered the
question "What is thy name?" with the proud words "Harry of Hereford, Lancaster, and Derby/ Am I," now tells the bitterness of banishment and the pain that comes from loss of those possessions and symbols which had heretofore guaranteed identity:

> Myself—a prince by fortune of my birth,
> Near to the King in blood, and near in love
> Till you did make him misinterpret me—
> Have stoop'd my neck under your injuries
> And sigh'd my English breath in foreign clouds,
> Eating the bitter bread of banishment,
> Whilst you have fed upon my signories,
> Dispark'd my parks and fell'd my forest woods,
> From my own windows torn my household coat,
> Raz'd out my imprese, leaving me no sign

Save men's opinions and my living blood
To show the world I am a gentleman.
                              (*Richard II*, III. i. 16–27)

Man has not merely lost his true identity for a time; he has, once he abandoned the old hierarchies and rituals, broken into a strange, new existence where he is free to slide back and forth along the vast scale of being, coming to rest momentarily at various points, but never knowing for certain just who and what he is, John of Gaunt's awkward punning on his name as he lies dying suggests the pervasiveness of the feeling that names and the identities they carry are no longer real and permanent but only the roles of the moment. This fluctuation in identity is the basic rhythm of the play, and we feel it everywhere, in Richard's ever-changing moods, in Bolingbroke's rising fortunes and changing names, in Richard's decline from King of England to his last appearance on stage, a body borne in by his murderer. The pattern of up-down, of restless change in the self, appears in its most complete form in the great final speech Richard gives, sitting in the dungeon of Pomfret Castle, about to die, and trying desperately to understand himself and this strange world into which he has fallen. Richard began as a great and secure king, seated on a throne, sure of himself, surrounded by pomp, confirmed by ceremony, looking out over a world of light where everything in the universe was open and ordered. At the end of the play he is the isolated individual, solitary, sitting in a small circle of light, surrounded by darkness and by a flinty prison wall, uncertain of any reality or truth. Isolated, like some hero of Kafka, in a mysterious and a containing world, Richard takes the confusing and conflicting evidence which his mind offers him and attempts, by means of reason and the poetic power to construct analogies, to "hammer it out," to give it shape and form, to achieve some new coherence. The results are not comforting. As hard as he hammers, he can discover only endless mutability in the life of man and endless restlessness in his soul. All evidence is now ambiguous: Where the Bible promises innocence an easy salvation in one passage, "come little ones," turn the page and it speaks in tragic tones of the passage to the Kingdom of Heaven being as difficult as a camel's threading the eye of a needle. Man's powers at one moment seem infinite and he feels that he can "tear a passage through the flinty ribs/ Of this hard world," but at the next moment he is the most helpless of creatures and can only comfort himself that many others have endured like misery. Fate forces new identities on him, but even in his own mind man can find no stability, and reality becomes theatrical, a playing of many roles in a constantly changing play:

> Thus play I in one person many people,
> And none contented. Sometimes am I king;
> Then treasons make me wish myself a beggar,
> And so I am. Then crushing penury
> Persuades me I was better when a king;
> Then am I king'd again; and by and by
> Think that I am unking'd by Bolingbroke,
> And straight am nothing. But whate'er I be,
> Nor I, nor any man that but man is,
> With nothing shall be pleas'd till he be eas'd
> With being nothing.
>
> *(Richard II,* V. v. 31–41)

To accommodate the newly perceived paradoxical, shifting reality Richard changes from the formal, conventional style of the beginning of the play to a metaphysical style capable of handling irony and a reality in which the parts no longer mesh, capable of carrying deep, intense agitation and the passionate effort of thought.

The world continues to speak ambiguously to Richard in the form of two visitors. The first is a poor groom from his stables who, having seen the King before only from a distance, now risks his life to come to speak of sympathy and duty which alters not when it alteration finds. The second visitor is the murderer Exton, who has come to kill Richard in hopes of reward from Henry. Richard, having tried to define himself by means of poetry and failed, now takes the way of drama, and acts. He seizes a sword from one of Exton's thugs and strikes two of them down before being killed himself. And so he defines himself in a dramatic or historic—not a philosophical—way. He has never solved the question whether he is king or beggar, never found the meaning he hoped to have; but he has stumbled through experience to quite a different answer. He, like the rest of men, has no stable identity certified by the order of things immutable. He is instead tragic man, whose identity fluctuates between hero and victim, king and corpse; whose values are not guaranteed by anything but his own willingness to die for them; whose life is a painful and continuing process of change. Richard traces the way that all other characters in this world must follow in their turn. . . .

Chronology of Important Dates

	Shakespeare	The Age
1564	Shakespeare born; christened at Stratford, April 26.	Death of Calvin. Marlowe born.
1567		Netherlands under William of Orange revolt against Spain.
1569		Catholic rising in England's north.
1570		Pope Pius excommunicates Queen Elizabeth.
1572		Massacre of St. Bartholomew's Day.
1582	Married to Anne Hathaway.	
1583	Daughter, Susanna, born.	
1587		Execution of Mary Stuart, Queen of Scots.
1588–1592	Early plays being performed in London. The three *Henry VI* plays, *The Comedy of Errors.*	Defeat of Spanish Armada (1588).
1593–1594	*Venus and Adonis* and *The Rape of Lucrece* dedicated to the Earl of Southampton. *Richard III, The Taming of the Shrew.*	Death of Marlowe (1593).
1595	*Richard II, A Midsummer-Night's Dream.*	
1596	*Romeo and Juliet.* Son, Hamnet, dies.	
1597	*Henry IV,* Parts I and II.	

1598		Edict of Nantes.
1599–1600	*Henry V, Julius Caesar, Twelfth Night.* Shakespeare's company moved to Globe Theatre.	Death of Spenser (1599).
1601–1602	*Hamlet, Troilus and Cressida.*	Essex Rebellion (1601).
1603–1604	*Measure for Measure, Othello.*	Queen Elizabeth's death and the accession of James I (1603).
1605–1606	*Macbeth, King Lear.*	Gunpowder Plot, led by Guy Fawkes (1605).
1607–1608	*Antony and Cleopatra, Coriolanus.*	Founding of the Jamestown Colony in Virginia (1607).
1609		Galileo builds a telescope in Padua.
1610–1611	*The Winter's Tale, The Tempest.* Shakespeare retired to Stratford.	Publication of the King James Version of the *Bible* (1611).
1616	Shakespeare died, April 23.	Death of Cervantes.
1623	*First Folio* published.	

Notes on the Editor and Contributors

PAUL M. CUBETA, the editor of this volume, is Professor of English and Academic Vice President of Middlebury College and Director of the Bread Loaf School of English. He is the editor of *Modern Drama for Analysis* and the author of essays on Jonson and Marlowe.

RICHARD D. ALTICK, Regents' Professor of English at Ohio State University, is the author of *The Art of Literary Research, Preface to Critical Reading,* and numerous publications on nineteenth-century English literature.

LEONARD F. DEAN is presently Professor of English at New York University. He has edited several collections of criticism, among them *Shakespeare: Modern Essays in Criticism.*

ALVIN B. KERNAN, a specialist in the English drama of the sixteenth and seventeenth centuries, is Professor of English at Yale University. He has written two books, *The Plot of Satire* and *The Cankered Muse,* and is also the editor of The Yale Ben Jonson, a projected series of seven volumes.

JAN KOTT, a member of the Polish resistance movement from 1942–1945, came to the United States in 1966. Author of *Shakespeare Our Contemporary,* he is Professor of Slavic Literature and Drama at the State University of New York, Stony Brook.

IRVING RIBNER became Chairman of the English Department, State University of New York, Stony Brook in 1968. His books include *The English History Play in the Age of Shakespeare* and *Patterns in Shakespearian Tragedy.*

BRENTS STIRLING, Professor Emeritus of English at the University of Washington, is the author of *The Populace of Shakespeare* and *A Shakespeare Sonnet Group.*

E. M. W. TILLYARD (1889–1962) is distinguished for his studies on the seventeenth century. He was Master of Jesus College at Cambridge, where he taught. Among his works are *Shakespeare's Last Plays, Shakespeare's History Plays,* and *The Elizabethan World Picture.*

DEREK TRAVERSI has served as British Council Representative for over twenty years. His first edition of *An Approach to Shakespeare,* 1938, made a major contribution to Shakespearean criticism. More recent works include *Shakespeare: The Last Phase* and *Shakespeare: The Roman Plays.*

PETER URE (1919–69) was Joseph Cowen Professor of English Language and Literature at the University of Newcastle upon Tyne. In addition to editing the Arden *Richard II*, he wrote *Shakespeare: The Problem Plays* and *Shakespeare and the Inward Self of the Tragic Hero.*

Selected Bibliography

Anderson, Ruth. "Kingship in Renaissance Drama." *Studies in Philology,* XLI (1944), 136–155. Informative background on Renaissance political theory.

Bogard, Travis. "Shakespeare's *Richard II*." PMLA, LXX (1955), 192–209. *Richard II* considered as an act of experimentation in which Shakespeare first becomes himself.

Dorius, R. J. "A Little More than a Little." *Shakespeare Quarterly,* XI (1960), 13–22. Excellent examination of imagery in *Richard II* and the Henry Plays.

Heninger, S. K., Jr. "The Sun-King Analogy in *Richard II*." *Shakespeare Quarterly,* XI (1960), 319–327. An attempt to reevaluate this most obvious of images in relation to thematic structure.

Knight, G. Wilson. "This Sceptered Isle." *The Sovereign Flower.* London: Methuen and Company, 1958. Illuminating look at the theme of divine authority versus the king's unsuitability.

Mahood, M. M. *Shakespeare's Wordplay.* London: Methuen and Company, 1957. In treating *Richard II,* Mahood argues that it is a play which questions the power of words.

Quinn, Michael. "The King Is Not Himself: The Personal Tragedy of Richard II." *Studies in Philology,* LVI (1959), 169–186. Asks whether *Richard II* is a tragedy or a history play by examining Richard's sense of identity.

Reiman, D. H. "Appearance, Reality, and Moral Order in *Richard II*." *Modern Language Quarterly,* XXV (1964), 34–45. Exposes the disparity between external words or actions and internal meaning or motive.

Suzman, Arthur. "Imagery and Symbolism in *Richard II*." *Shakespeare Quarterly,* VII (1956), 355–370. Demonstrates the correspondence between Shakespeare's imagery and action.

Tillyard, E. M. W. *The Elizabethan World Picture.* New York: The Macmillan Company, 1944. *Richard II* as an example of the Great Chain of Being.

Traversi, Derek. *Shakespeare from Richard II to Henry V.* Stanford, California: Stanford University Press, 1957. One of the best critical studies of Shakespeare's Second Tetralogy.

Whitaker, Virgil. *The Mirror Up to Nature.* San Marino, California: Huntington Library, 1965. Succinct analysis of the structural weaknesses in the play.

Wilson, J. Dover. *The Essential Shakespeare.* Cambridge: Cambridge University Press, 1932. Richard II as an immature Lear.

Wilson, J. Dover, ed. *Richard II.* Cambridge: Cambridge University Press, 1939. Contains vigorous, authoritative, and well-researched discussion of sources.

Yeats, William Butler. "At Stratford-on-Avon." From *Essays and Introductions.* New York: The Macmillan Company, 1961; London: Macmillan and Company, Ltd., 1961. Explication of Richard through the endlessly reverberating implications of Yeats' own metaphors.